Adam & Eve
&
The Big Bang

Peter Leadley

ISBN: 978-90-818798-1-1

DEDICATION

To the one hundred and ten billion souls who preceded us

CONTENTS

ACKNOWLEDGMENTS

Ivanhoe 1963 & Yoni A for their Hebrew

Pastor Mark Oortman for his critique of my method.

Smithsonian Institute Human Origins Program, Washington, USA for their 'hairless primate' explanation

Wesley Meijer for his technical knowledge and generosity.

And all my friends and family who refrained from calling me a fool for attempting this!

.

1 INTRODUCTION

The biggest problem with Life is that you don't really begin to understand it until you're almost through it. All those years of living, working and just carrying on as best you can, suddenly seem to be a bit of a waste. Just as you come to the realisation that you have a handle on it, it hits you that it's almost too late to enjoy it for what it is!

Look into the night sky above your head. Better still get on a plane and fly to Agadir[5] in Morocco, then get the bus to L'Ayoun[46], way down in the Sahara desert. With a couple of litres of water, a loaf of bread and half a kilo of dates in your rucksack, walk for about ten kilometres south of the town. Wait until one o' clock in the morning, and then look into the night sky above your head. Unless you are a frequent visitor to the great deserts of the world, where light pollution does not infringe upon the natural beauty of the night sky, you will be greeted by a sight that will simply astonish you. Scattered like diamonds across a sky of black velvet, there are more stars than the soul can comprehend. Try and take in the awesome beauty of it. Then sit there and wait for the magical kaleidoscope that is a Saharan dawn.

Sometime after the awe begins to fade, travel to Egypt, and witness a Red Sea Sunset at the place known as Ras Mohammed[59]. Watch the dying rays of the Sun turn the Red Sea, the Sinai Desert and the Sinai Mountains, to a blood red. This is a sunset that defies belief in its scope and magnificence. According to many travel brochures, you will have witnessed one of nature's greatest spectacles. They may well be right. This and the Saharan night sky are two memories that will stay with me until I die; two of the most beautiful things I have ever witnessed.

There is, however, another miracle that is not so obvious to the average man, but is far more exciting to his intellect. Himself. Just standing there scratching your bum, you represent one of the greatest mysteries that has ever confronted mankind. Where did we come from? Who are we? Allied to this, the bigger question: where did the Universe[76] come from?

Men have struggled to answer these two problems for thousands of years. A hundred thousand years ago, a man sat on a log in the entrance to his cave looking out into the darkness of the night, and for a moment, his attention strayed from watching for the ever present predators, to the twinkling stars above him. He too wondered, 'How?' Millennia later the Egyptian priests and scholars tried to explain to their Pharaoh just what it was that he looked at when he stood on the terrace of his palace in Thebes, watching the stars as they slowly travelled across the night sky. Then the Greeks, the Persians, the Romans, the Islamic scholars, the Papal astronomers; they all pondered that greatest of all mysteries. Where did it all come from?

One day, (October 4, 1957), the Soviet Union launched the first man-made object ever to leave the Earth and go into the vastness of space. Sputnik 1 was the first tentative step towards solving the riddle. It was the beginning of a new era. Everyone knew of the others. The Stone Age[73], the Bronze Age[13], and the Iron Age[39], and the sometimes referred to modern era called the Steam Age[72]. Now a new and exciting era was upon us, the Space Age[70]; and with it came the realisation that we had the opportunity to find out more about the history of the Universe than ever before. Sure enough, scientists soon had satellites whizzing around the planet looking down on the Earth, and up into the Cosmos[76]. Every day seemed to bring new revelations about the Great Unknown. Dan Dare and Flash Gordon stopped being just fantasy, and suddenly represented every little boy's dream of becoming an Astronaut.

It is true that many amazing things have been discovered and that we now know far more about the Universe than we ever did before; but even as new and more powerful tools are employed on this great quest, there are more new questions arising than there are answers being discovered to old ones.

There is also a great debate raging between two seemingly opposed schools of thought, the Scientific and the Religious. I've wondered for many years about religion and spirituality, about science and physics. Being neither an academic, nor a theologian, I struggled to understand their differing viewpoints until one day, in 1986, whilst scuba diving in the Gulf of Aqaba[7]. In those days tourists were a rarity in Sinai; the roads quiet and the nights starlit havens of tranquility. Looking back I realise how fortunate I was to experience its unspoiled beauty.

I was contemplating the coral reef known as 'The Temple', when the penny finally dropped and I saw what life was all about. What *is* the meaning of Life, the Universe and Everything? Not, I can assure you, '42' as 'Deep Thought'* would have you believe. Mind you, from an atheist[4] perspective, that's as good an answer as any, but for some of us, a little more detail is necessary. Ever since Charles Darwin published his theory that every living creature has, and continues to evolve from a single common source, there has been fierce debate between the 'Creationists' (those who support Religious accounts of creation) and the 'Darwinists' (those who support Darwin's theory of Evolution).

This book is my humble attempt to examine the aforementioned question; where did we, and it, all come from. Not that I put my musings on the same level of the late and much missed Douglas Adams, but I flatter myself by thinking that I may actually have something to say, adding my two cents worth to the great debate.

Is there a God[25]? Was there a Big Bang[10]? Did Darwin really hit on the answer to the question, 'Where did we come from?' Now I see the subject matter in front of me on the page, I must admit my confidence ebbs a little. These are the greatest mysteries that mankind has ever pondered. Can I really add something of value to the quest for the truth? Probably not, and I'm bound to get an argument, but everyone's entitled to their opinion......even me.

As you will no doubt observe if you do me the honour of

reading this digest, just as fascinating as the history of our planet and ourselves; are the religious accounts and legends that have evolved along with mankind. Bearing in mind that most religious texts are legend, we have to accept that (being a legend) there is hidden *somewhere* in the story, a grain of truth at least.

I've set out to try and compare and reconcile some of the differences that exist between the religious communities and the scientific ones as to how human life on Earth came about, and where the Earth itself sprang from. How the Universe appeared and what is its destiny. Both schools of thought have their own pet theories and arguments, many of which are very complicated and sophisticated. I don't intend to get too involved in the details and machinations of quantum physics or theological philosophy, or at least, not if I can avoid it.

Keeping it simple and in layman's terms seems like a good idea to me, after all, that's just what I am, a simple layman[47].

Religion and Science doesn't have to be an either/or situation. You can, as did Darwin[14] and Newton[51], have faith in both of them. So here we have a sort of Idiot's Guide to Life the Universe and Everything'. Please bear in mind that I am going to examine various passages in the Old Testament and compare them with each other and also with scientific and historical facts to determine if they are themselves based on fact. I have used the Oxford University Press reproduction of the King James Authorised Version of 1611 as my reference. It is the oldest translation of the Hebrew and Aramaic texts into English and as such is not corrupted as are later versions of it written in modern colloquial English.

This is not an exercise in proving or disproving the existence of a supreme deity. I am not some sort of Biblical apologist. I have assumed both science and the Bible to have a certain element of truth in them to enable their statements to be compared.

So where do we start? Do we deal with the logical first step, that of the creation of the Universe and everything in it, or shall we be indulge our all too human trait and be narcissistic? Let's look at our favourite subject first. Ourselves

2 ADAM & EVE: THE ODD COUPLE

Let's   start with the legend. The beginning of our species was, according to the Biblical Scriptures, Adam and Eve. Their story is told in the Book of Genesis, the first book of the Christian Bible and the Jewish Torah. Whilst these are not the oldest written historical documents, they are by far and away the most famous. Genesis doesn't state when it was written, or by whom, but according to many religious analysts, the likely date of its authorship is between 1440 and 1400 B.C., between the time Moses led the Israelites out of Egypt and his death on Mount Nebo in Jordan.

It was, supposedly, Moses that commissioned the first five books of the Bible. They are: Genesis, Exodus, Leviticus, Numbers and Deuteronomy. The Book of Exodus, or at least the parts pertaining to him, must also be considered a biography of Moses' life. As a Prince of Egypt, Moses may have been able to write, but it has to be considered that the alphabet of Egypt, where he would have been educated as a boy, was hieroglyphics. Presumably, most of his time after the Exodus from Egypt would be taken up with his responsibility of leading/governing the Tribes of Israel so the actual writing was sub-contracted out.

Apparently two scribes had spent the time the Tribes of Israel were wandering around the deserts of the Middle East, penning this illustrious History of Man in Hebrew and Aramaic. Scholars generally agree that it is the work of more than one person, as there are two distinct styles of writing in it. Given the fact that the time span of its authorship covers some forty years, it is probably a labour of love by two or more dedicated scholars of the time.

It really is the 'Greatest Story Ever Told'.

The main characters in the story of the Creation of Man are Adam, Eve his wife, and their two sons, Cain and Able. There are others, but their celebrity pales to insignificance compared to our Odd Couple and their offspring.

Just in case you're not familiar with the legend of the Original Couple, or your memory needs refreshing, here's what the Bible has to say about it.

Holy Bible (King James Version) Genesis 1:26-2:1

1:26 And God said, Let us make man in our image, after our likeness: and let them have dominion over the fish of the sea, and over the fowl of the air, and over the cattle, and over all the earth, and over every creeping thing that creepeth upon the earth.

1:27 So God created man in his own image, in the image of God created he him; **male and female created he them**.

1:28 And God blessed them, and God said unto them, be fruitful, and multiply, and <u>replenish the earth</u>, and subdue it: and have dominion over the fish of the sea, and over the fowl of the air, and over every living thing that moveth upon the earth.

1:29 And God said, Behold, I have given you every <u>herb bearing seed</u>, which is upon the face of all the earth, and *every tree, in which is the fruit of a tree yielding seed; to you it shall be for meat.*

1:30 and to every beast of the earth, and to every fowl of the air, and to everything that creepeth upon the earth, wherein there is life, I have given every green herb for meat: and it was so.

1:31 And God saw everything that he had made, and, behold, it was very good. And the evening and the morning were the sixth day.

2:1 Thus, the heavens and the earth were finished and all the host of them.

So there you have it. May I point out that in these seven verses there is evidence that a vegetarian and sustainable lifestyle is required? No greenhouse gas producing animals farmed for meat, and everything used to be replenished. Climate change avoided. Should have listened folks.

Obviously some considerable time had passed between the time of Adam and Eve and the writing down of their story. We can never know how much time had elapsed between the creation of the Odd Couple and the penning of their story but according to one very dedicated and enthusiastic Bishop Usher (1581-1656), Archbishop of Armagh, and Anglican Primate of all Ireland, Adam and Eve were driven from Paradise by God on Monday 10 November 4004 BC. This would mean that in his view, some 2560 to 2580 years had passed between the Eviction and the publication of Genesis.

This remarkable statement was made after Archbishop Usher had spent most of his life working through the generations of men referred to in the first books of the Bible. They are listed in many places, and most have their age at their death, or the number of years that had passed since another stated date, e.g., the birth of a child or the death of a father, etc.

There it is a comprehensive description of the Creation of Mankind. Please note that there is nowhere in this description, any reference to whom God is referring when he creates 'male and female' nor for the benefit of those of you who know the story, is there any mention of God creating Eve from Adam's rib. It simply states that He made male and female. It does imply, however, that they were created at the same time. Later on Genesis tells us Adam and Eve were the sole (human) occupants of the Garden of Eden and that God commanded them not to 'Eat of the Fruit of the Tree of Knowledge of Good and Evil'. Eve was persuaded by the snake (Satan) to eat of the forbidden fruit and then to give some to her husband. This she duly did, but when God found out what they had done, he expelled them from the Garden of Eden.

The expulsion, we are told, was to prevent them finding the Tree of Life, and eating of its fruit as well, making them, 'like us', that is, immortal. Divinities, it seems, are rather worried about us humans finding the key to immortality.

Whilst Genesis is undoubtedly extremely old, it is not the oldest known written story. These are from 2600BC and are

Sumerian texts from Abu Salabikh, which include the 'Instructions of Shuruppak' and the 'Kesh Temple Hymn'. The Epic of Gilgamesh, who was the fifth king of Uruk, (modern day Iraq) is from about 2500 BC., and I use quotations from it as it contains information that is mirrored in The Book of Genesis.

The 'Epic of Gilgamesh', tells of King Gilgamesh and his adopted brother, Enkidu. There is a reference to mankind seeking immortality here too. Gilgamesh attempts to learn the secret of eternal life after Enkidu is killed. He does this by undertaking a long and perilous journey to meet the immortal flood hero, Utnapishtim. The advice given to Gilgamesh by Siduri (the "woman of the vine"), whom he encounters on the way, has become the most widely known excerpt from the Epic.

"Gilgamesh, whither are you wandering? Life, which you look for, you will never find. For when the gods created man, they let death be his share, and life withheld in their own hands.

Gilgamesh, fill your belly, day and night make merry, let your days be full of joy, dance and make music day and night. And wear fresh clothes, and wash your head and bathe. Look at the child that is holding your hand, and let your wife delight in your embrace. These things alone are the concern of men."

This seems to be independent verification that immortality is the sole domain of the Divine, which, when we consider our own brief lives, is undeniable. Surprisingly, this earthy advice given by Siduri is also repeated in the Bible.

Holy Bible (King James Version) Luke 12:19

12:19 And I will say to my soul, Soul, thou hast much goods laid up for many years; take thine ease, eat, drink, and be merry.

In 1st Corinthians 15:32 it adds 'for tomorrow we may die'. Much the same thing is repeated in Ecclesiastes 8:15, and Isaiah 22:12. This is truly a very old philosophy indeed and one that has a lot going for it. I shall do my best to comply.

But I digress. Let's get back to the Odd Couple. For Adam and Eve it seems ignorance was indeed bliss. Made by God from clay and having life breathed into him, Adam became our common ancestor and, controversially, (believe it or not) according to Genesis Chapter 2, verses 21-22, the source of all women. Eve, fashioned from one of Adam's ribs, became his companion and helper.

Holy Bible (King James Version) Genesis 2:21-25

²¹And the LORD God caused a deep sleep to fall upon Adam, and he slept: and he took one of his ribs, and closed up the flesh instead thereof;

²² And the rib, which the LORD God had taken from man, made he a woman, and brought her unto the man.

*²³ And Adam said, This is **now** bone of my bones, and flesh of my flesh: she shall be called Woman, because she was taken* *out of Man.*

²⁴ Therefore shall a man leave his father and his mother, and shall cleave unto his wife: and they shall be one flesh.

²⁵ And they were both naked, the man and his wife, and were not ashamed.

This would be a good story in those days and quite sufficient to explain our presence, especially in the absence of any reason to doubt it. However, don't dismiss it as just a fairy tale. There are some remarkable statements hiding in these ancient writings.

Made from clay? Not possible? You've heard the expression, 'You are what you eat'? Well, it's based on the assumption that a human body is the sum total of its input, minus expelled material. The retained bits are the food that our bodies use to build us and fuel our activity. So just where does the clay come in then? For the answer to this question we must look at where our food (vegetarian as prescribed in Genesis 1:29) originates, and how it affects us.

Take the potato, the humble spud. It grows in the ground and when harvested soon makes its way onto our plates. But consider for a moment the potato's growing process. Drawing water and its own food from the surrounding soil, it uses the nutrients drawn from the earth to fuel its own growth, so, without mother earth it would be nowhere. Totally dependent on the soil it grows in for its existence. By extension the person who consumes the potato is also reliant upon those nutrients for their existence, making us 'made from clay' in a not too roundabout way.

'All very well', I hear you say, 'but that's just a coincidence, an accident of the writing.' Maybe, but how many coincidences can you get in a few lines of an old book?

Eve and Dolly the Sheep

Here's another 'coincidence'. How about making a woman from a rib? Well, surprisingly, there is a very solid basis for this. Taking material from one animal and manually making another from it, that is, by a-sexual (without sexual intercourse) reproduction; is known as 'cloning'.

The story of the rib and the creation of Eve is a remarkable parallel description of cloning. It happens that reproduction of an animal with no 'Y' chromosome will result in a female. The 'Y' chromosome is donated only by sperm. The male's sperm cells in humans and other mammals contain one of two types of sex chromosomes. They are called either 'X' or 'Y'. The female's eggs, however, contain only the X chromosome. The gender of a baby is determined by which of the chromosomes join together during conception. If a sperm cell containing an X chromosome fertilizes an egg, the resulting baby will be X+X or female. If the sperm cell contains a Y chromosome, then the resulting baby will be X+Y or male. As you can see, without the sexual donation of a Y chromosome, the feminine gender will be the 'default' situation like Dolly the sheep*, and Eve, the first woman.

*Dolly the Sheep: (5 July 1996–14 Feb 2003) cloned at the Roslin Institute, Scotland

This is a hugely simplified version of this particular discipline of science (genetics) the practitioners of which study DNA[15a] and have decoded (beginning Crick and Watson) the human 'Genome'. This is the chemical binary code that is written into all living creature's cells, to ensure that the correct biological information is passed on during reproduction. It is because of the outstanding work done by these researchers that we have so much knowledge about our origins. It's a science that is far and away more complicated than the rocket variety.

So why take a rib? What's so special about that? The Genesis account may be an ancient explanation for the absence of an entirely different bone. Most male mammals and all male primates have a Baculum[9], a bone for stiffening the penis as an aid to copulation. Humans however, do not. We are the exception that relies purely on blood pressure to do the job, which, incidentally, strikes me as putting us men at something of a distinct disadvantage.

The verse describing the creation of Eve relates that Adam has a bone removed from his body, and that he refers to his newly made mate as a blood relative. He considers her such because he says she is **'now'** bone of my bones and flesh of my flesh', which is a common description of a close family relative. We have to take into account the translation factor here. Being an English speaker, and not being able to read Biblical Hebrew, I have had to turn to translations of the old scriptures for my information.

The oldest English translation I have been able to obtain,

and therefore probably the most accurate is called the King James Version. In 1604, King James 1st of England commissioned a new translation of the Bible into English from the original Hebrew and Aramaic in which it was written. It was completed in 1611. Being nearest to the original, it is the one least likely to have had anything changed.

However, this is the point where we come to problems with translations. Much is dependent upon the translator's own idea of what is being said, as opposed to what is actually being said. Every translated document is exposed to the 'Chinese Whisper' syndrome. When something difficult to translate comes up, the translator has to put in what he *thinks* is correct, and it may not always be what the original author wanted.

Biblical scribes never use the word penis or vagina. It is conservative to the point of being comical when dealing with indelicate matters such as sex, hence all the 'knowing' of wives, to whom men 'go into'. Some scholars suggest that the story of Eve's creation is an explanatory myth to explain the absence of a Baculum in the human male, rather than a missing rib. Contrary to popular myth, men and women have an identical number of ribs in their ribcage, so one would have to assume that the 'rib' did not come from here.

It would be very symbolic, using this part of the male anatomy (Baculum) to create new life. Most appropriate. The closing of flesh mentioned in Genesis 2:21 would then refer to the 'raphe', a seam on the penis and scrotum. If indeed, the missing Baculum was the bone used in the creation of Eve, using the word 'Rib' would be a logical thing to do. It is often used in Hebrew from which the Genesis was translated, to denote something used to stiffen a construction, such as the 'rib' of a boat. Again, most appropriate.

This information was all translated from the original Hebrew text. As I said, I'm no theologian, so I make no apology for my Hebrew illiteracy. A little later on you will find some Hebrew, and its translation, but which, alas, was not done by me. So far we have a similarity between fact and legend. I know many of you would argue that you don't believe that the Bible is authentic, or don't believe in the existence of a superior being or deity, but bear with me on this. You don't have to believe in anything except your own ability to think. Remember what we are dealing with are the writings of men who lived thousands of years before most people could read and write, let alone study embryology or genetics.

We shall be coming to the harder evidence a little later. What we have to do is to keep an open mind and try to make something positive out of the myriad of conjecture, myth and legend. OK? Good!

The Ex- Wife

Many of us, myself included, have a first, failed union, which we have put behind us and moved on. So, it appears, is the case with Adam. Let me introduce you to his ex, a lady who went by the name of Lilith.

It's more than likely that you may have heard of her before, but not in a Biblical context. Here we come across one of those little mentioned episodes that seem to be a bit of a paradox or sometimes a seeming embarrassment to the various churches and theologians. Indeed, poor old Lilith is left out of the Bible completely, but for one short but very vague possible reference in Isaiah, where she may be referred to as 'the great owl'.

Holy Bible (King James Version) Isaiah 34.14 – 15

34:14 The wild beasts of the desert shall also meet with the wild beasts of the island, and the satyr shall cry to his fellow; the screech owl also shall rest there, and find for herself a place of rest.

*34:15 There shall **the great owl** make her nest, and lay, and hatch, and gather under her shadow: there shall the vultures also be gathered, everyone with her mate.*

This is a very loosely translated version of the Hebrew, and is somewhat different in later Bibles. Here, it is difficult to see any reference to Lilith as the translators and scribes were extremely reluctant to use the names of any creature from mythology, considering them to be Un-Christian, or Pagan in origin. The name 'Lilith' only appears in modern translations of the Bible. But where does she come from? The first reference to a female other than Eve being created is in the following verse.

Holy Bible (King James Version) Genesis 1:27

1:27 So God created man in his own image, in the image of God created he him; male and female created he them.

She was created equal, but different and, please note, apparently at the same time as Adam. No mention of the famous rib incident, and crucially she was made at the same moment as the male. Now, assuming the male in question is indeed Adam, his mate has been made from the 'dust of the Earth', as he was. Not from a rib. However, the first chapter of Genesis is one description of the 'Creation' ending with the sixth day, and in Chapter Two is a more detailed description, but only of the creation of Humans and the Garden of Eden.

It should be noted that Adam does not name his new found mate until Chapter Three. This is of interest because the style of writing changes here, reverting to the same style as used in Chapter One. Could it be that two differing accounts were used, or do we have a 'two women' situation?

There will be those that argue that the creation of Eve is referred to in Chapter One and that the later passage just gives the detail of it. The trouble is of course, it doesn't read that way, and what is the point of having scriptures if you don't read them the way they were written? You either read it as it is, or the whole thing becomes a meaningless train of conjecture.

This original couple (Adam and Lilith) were created quite a

while before Adam is put into a deep sleep and operated upon to produce Eve.

Holy Bible (King James Version) Genesis 2:21

2:21 And the LORD God caused a deep sleep to fall upon Adam, and he slept: and he took one of his ribs, and closed up the flesh instead thereof;

2:22 And the rib, which the LORD God had taken from man, made he a woman, and brought her unto the man.

*2:23 And Adam said, <u>This is **now** bone of my bones, and flesh of my flesh</u>: she shall be called Woman, because she was taken out of Man.*

The big thing here is that Adam says that his new woman is '**now** bone of my bones', which infers that some previous thing wasn't. That something else could only be the first female whose creation from clay is described in Genesis 1:26-27. This description differs from the creation of Eve at Genesis 2:21-22 who was created from one of Adam's ribs, whereas the first creation of a female was from 'dust', or more correctly, from earth or soil. Just to show you how translation can skew the story, let's look at the original Hebrew text. Here's the original and a literal translation. Please note, not dust, but 'earth' or 'soil'. The word 'clay' is a better choice than 'dust'.

וַיִּיצֶר - created (singular masculine):

יְהוָה אֱלֹהִים – God:

אֶת-הָאָדָם - the man (direct object):

עָפָר - earth, soil:

מִן – from :

הָאֲדָמָה - the earth:

וַיִּפַּח - and he blew (wind, breath):

בְּאַפָּיו - in his nostrils:

נִשְׁמַת - breath of:

חַיִּים – life:

וַיְהִי – became:

הָאָדָם - the man:

לְנֶפֶשׁ - to a soul:

חַיָּה – living.

You have the word formed by the Hebrew word "yasar" which means to be literally forged or formed or sculpted. Thus we see that man was not a simple lump of clay but was a work of art by God. It is here we have "apar" which is translated in the King James Version as 'dust' but is actually 'soil'. Continuing, "nesamah" which means a breath or a blast of wind, sometimes referred to as spirit, and then "nepes". God made man a living soul, one that was alive, independent of that which is required to be sustained by another.

Small additions, changes and emissions can make a huge difference to a translation. In many Bibles, especially 'Modern' translations, Genesis 2:23 has been presented as *'this is bone of my bones...'* omitting the word 'now', which alters the meaning completely. The word 'now' brings to light the possibility that something preceding Eve wasn't bone of his bones, but **now** Eve is. Leaving the word out completely removes the possible existence of Lilith. This bolsters the agenda of those clerics that refute the equality of women, or would wish to remove Lilith from the story because of her demonic and un-savoury qualities. Her refusal to submit to Adam would mean that God had made a mistake in creating her, allowing the common man and the non-believer to question the infallibility and divinity of God. Not a situation that any of the Abrahamic religions could tolerate as it would demean and devalue their reason for being.

We must ask ourselves why is the creation of woman written down twice, in different circumstances and from differing materials, unless there are two different women? It may look at first reading that this is a second description of the same occurrence, but why should there be two (different) accounts of the same thing? It happens nowhere else in the Bible.

This is where the 'first wife' theory comes in. Jewish folklore, (and you must remember that Genesis is a Jewish Scripture) from the 8th–10th Century 'Alphabet of Ben Sira', Lilith is Adam's first wife or partner, who was created at the same time and from the same earth as Adam.

While God created Adam, who was alone, He said, 'It is not good for man to be alone' He also created a woman, from the earth, as He had created Adam himself, and called her Lilith. Adam and Lilith immediately began to fight. She said, 'I will not lie below,' and he said, 'I will not lie beneath you, but only on top.'

According to the Jewish writings, Lilith and Adam came to a parting of the ways when she refused to be subservient to him. Made from the same clay or dust as Adam and being made equal and not subservient to him, Lilith, as Ben Sira calls her, goes on to suffer the same fate as Satan, and ends up being cursed. The legend was greatly developed during the Middle Ages, in the tradition of Aggadic Midrashim, the Zohar and Jewish mysticism.

In the 13th Century writings of Rabbi Isaac ben Jacob Alfasi ha-Cohen, for example, Lilith left Adam after she refused to become subservient to him. Then she wouldn't return to the Garden of Eden after she mated with the Archangel Samael, whom, incidentally is considered by many to be the fallen angel whom we know as Satan or Iblis, the Devil himself. The result of their union was the multiplicity of demons in the Christian tradition, which are known as Djinn in the Islamic world. Presumably Lilith and Samael did it standing up....

The Lilith legend is still commonly used as source material in modern Western culture, literature, occultism, fantasy, and horror. The name Lilith, because of its demonic connections, is not one commonly used as a girl's name.

Jezebel, Delilah and Salome are also names with infamous connotations that are very rarely used because of Biblical stories. Not that the situation is peculiar to the fair sex. Who would name their son Judas?

There are other cultures referring to Lilith, or to a creature identical to her. Labartu (in Sumerian Dimme) was a very similar Mesopotamian demon to Lilith, and Lilith seems to have inherited many of Labartu's myths. She was considered a demi-goddess and daughter of Anu, the sky god. Many incantations against her mention her status as a 'daughter of heaven' and her exercising her free will over infants. This makes her different from the rest of the demons in Mesopotamia. Unlike her peers, Labartu was not instructed by the gods to do evil; she did it of her own accord, uniquely exercising 'free will', which was the gift we are led to believe, God gave solely to Adam and Mankind.

Labartu seduced men, harmed pregnant women, mothers and neonates, killed foliage and drank blood and was a cause of disease, sickness and death. The space between her legs is denoted as a scorpion, corresponding to the astrological sign of Scorpio. (Scorpio rules the genitals and sex organs.) Her head is that of a lion and she has bird's feet. Her breasts are suckled by a pig and a dog, and she rides on the back of a donkey.

Lilith as a person is not, unfortunately, of much interest to us in these musings. As a mythical character and possibly the first woman and intended partner for Adam, she is fascinating, but plays no real part in the propagation of the species, which is all down to Eve, bless her. All of which is a pity really, because I like a feisty woman.

I feel that it is essential to point out this 'ex-wife' or 'Lilith' theory to those who may not be aware of it, as we now go on to look at the possibility of other females who may have lived during this period of time, and later on, the fact that Eve must have had at least two daughters.

Make a cup of coffee, we deserve one.

3 CAIN & ABLE & THE KIDS

Many who wish to discredit the Biblical scriptures ask, 'If Adam and Eve were the originators of the whole population of Humans, then where did their sons, Cain and Able, find their wives?'

Good point. If Adam and Eve were original and unique, there could be no eligible wives. There is no mention of daughters being born to Eve, just sons. The expansion of the human race would have come to an abrupt halt, and this book would be neither appropriate nor possible. So what happened? Where *did* the breeding stock come from?

The first and most famous murder in all of history takes place here. Cain kills Able, forever condemning himself in the eyes of the world. No offspring from Able then. Cain goes on to move house to the Land of Nod, (no, not the one in East Yorkshire, UK) and marries a girl who's name we are not told.

"Nod" (נוד) is the Hebrew root of the verb "to wander" (לנדוד).

Therefore, to dwell in the land of Nod means to live a wandering or nomadic life. This is obviously a reference to the lifestyle of early Humans, who were hunter gatherers. So whilst Cain may seem to be a mythical figure, he accurately represents the earliest human population.

Now for the Million dollar Question. Where did Cain find his wife? There are of course, references in Genesis to other people, but no explanation as to where they came from or who they were. A casual reference to other humans, or their like, brings up the suggestion of other people being present at the time of the original couple. The first of these is....

Holy Bible (King James Version) Genesis 4:16-17

4:16 And Cain went out from the presence of the LORD, and dwelt in the land of Nod, on the east of Eden.

4:17 And Cain knew his wife; and she conceived, and bare Enoch: and he builded a city, and called the name of the city, after the name of his son, Enoch.

This is closely followed by....

Holy Bible (King James Version) Genesis 4:18-25

4:18 And unto Enoch was born Irad; and Irad begot Mehujael; and Mehujael begot Methushael; and Methushael begot Lamech.

4:19 And Lamech took unto him two wives; the name of one was Adah, and the name of the other Zillah.

4:20 And Adah bore <u>Jabal; he was the father of such as dwell in tents and have cattle.</u>

4:21 And his brother's name was Jubal; he was the father of all such as handle the harp and pipe.

*4:22 And Zillah, she also bore **Tubal-cain**<u>, the forger of every</u>*
<u>*cutting instrument of brass and iron;*</u> *and the sister of Tubal-*
cain was Naamah.

4:23 And Lamech said unto his wives: Adah and Zillah, hear
my voice; ye wives of Lamech, hearken unto my speech; for I
have slain a man for wounding me, and a young man for
bruising me;

4:24 If Cain shall be avenged sevenfold, truly Lamech
seventy and sevenfold.

4:25 And Adam knew his wife again; and she bore a son,
and called his name Seth: 'for God hath appointed me
another seed instead of Abel; for Cain slew him".

The whole thing seems a little odd. How can there be all these other people around if Adam and Eve were the first humans and Cain was their only surviving child? Well, obviously, they were not. There was Lilith for one, but Adam and Lilith never got around to doing the business and producing potential wives for Cain because they couldn't agree on who should do what or to whom.....

It is often suggested that Incest is a possibility, provided of course, that Eve gave birth to daughters. One must assume that as Adam and Eve's genes were perfect, as they were 'new' so to speak; there was no possibility of damaging recessive genes surfacing and spoiling the future of Mankind. According to Genesis, Eve had no daughters that we know of, at least until after Seth was born, and that is *after* Cain took a wife, so it rules out the possibility of any incestuous relationships.

There is no family referred to in the Bible for the mother of Enoch to have come from either. There are eight men and three wives referred to in this passage, as well as the two men with whom Lamech fought, and yet as far as Genesis is concerned, no other people have been produced. Eve gives birth again *after* these events, (to Seth) providing evidence that these things were all happening at approximately the same time, or at least during the alleged 930 years of Adam's allotted lifespan.

However, we must get back to the first born. Cain must have looked outside his own family circle for his mate, but where? The clues are there, but, like Cain, we have to look outside the scriptures for the answers. Whilst Cain's infamous fall from grace is well documented, a much shorter passage in Genesis gives us an indication to what the situation actually was. Here we have the much debated 'Sons of God'.

Holy Bible (King James Version) Genesis 6:1

6:1 And it came to pass, when men began to multiply on the face of the earth, and daughters were born unto them,

6:2 That the **sons of God** *saw the* **daughters of men** *that they were fair; and they took them wives of all which they chose.*

6:3 And the LORD said, My spirit shall not always strive with man, for that he also is flesh: yet his days shall be an hundred and twenty years.

*6:4 **<u>There were giants in the earth in those days</u>**; and also after that, when the sons of God came in unto the daughters of men, and they bare children to them, the same became mighty men **<u>which were of old, men of renown.</u>***

Now, apart from causing confusion about the Christian Holy Trinity, (God the Father, God the Son, and God the Holy Spirit, three entities in one) this passage also indicates the presence of other people on the Earth. Just who could the 'Sons of God' possibly be, and who did men have, to 'multiply' with? I have highlighted the parts in the passage that are of most interest to us at this point. It really is an enlightening and very important passage. The few lines above actually explain the origins of the mysterious wives.

In Genesis 4:17, Cain 'knows' his wife, in the Biblical sense. Unfortunately we don't 'know' her in the literal sense. Where did she come from and where does Enoch find someone to bear Irad? Presumably Irad's wife was from the same community that his son, Mehujael, and his grandson Lamech, (who had at least two wives) got theirs.

It's all very puzzling, don't you think? Unless of course you admit there were other humans knocking about who aren't mentioned, or indeed, are not 'human' in the same way as Adam and Eve. But who was not human like Adam and Eve? The answer, if we take a look at the scientific school of thought is fairly obvious. Remember, the object of this exercise is to cross reference sources of information to try and highlight similarities between the two schools of thought. Or facilitate a compromise. Or (if we're lucky) get another argument going!

*6:2 That the **sons of God saw the daughters of men** that they were fair; and they took them wives of all which they chose.*

We have to consider descriptions of parentage here. A male is usually created by his father and mother but as Adam was the creation of God, it's only reasonable to call him the son of God. Equally any other male created by God could also be called the son of God. But why refer to them in this manner? It's to differentiate between Adam, who is a man as we are and the other males who were not. They were still, according to the writers of Genesis, sons of God, but not the same as Adam.

Adam we would recognise as a Homo sapien. The others therefore must have been one of the other sub species of Hominin that were living when H.sapien (legendary Adam) first arose. They would be H.heidelbergensis or H.erectus. Both are of the primate genus Homo, and could interbreed with H.sapiens. That the writers of Genesis knew of the existence of other humans is incredible, as they were separated in time by at least 75,000 years. That stories told around a campfire at night could accurately pass information down through the generations for that amount of time, until the Hebrew scribes would write them down seems impossible. However, let me bring your attention to the Australian Aborigines 'Dreamtime'.

The Dreamtime is the period referred to in the stories told by the native Australians, describing their origins and how they came about. It is the native Australians equivalent of the story of Creation in Genesis. It is not generally well understood by non-indigenous Australians, but the story goes something like this.

The Dreamtime was way back, at the very beginning of time. The land and the people were created by the Spirits who made the rivers, streams, water holes the land, hills, rocks, plants and animals. The Spirits gave them their hunting tools and each tribe its land, their totems and their Dreaming. The entire world was made by their Ancestors way back in the very beginning of time, the Dreamtime.

My apologies to my Australian brothers and sisters for my crudity describing their sacred beliefs and for disseminating them, but the principles followed in this book demand that all Creation stories be treated as equals.

Fossilised human footprints have shown that humans were present in Australia by about 50 to 60,000 years ago, and DNA sequencing, puts the earliest Native Australian presence about the same time. The same DNA sequencing shows that the original Australians were immigrants from Indonesia and they probably first set foot in Arnhemland in the Northern Territories, virtually right where the sacred Dreamtime rock paintings are. So here we have an ancient sacred folk tale, the Dreamtime, accurate to within a few kilometres, 60,000 years after the event. Science and religion hand in hand and as accurate as you could wish for. Why then, should the folk tales that Moses' scribes wrote down be any less accurate?

So which of our two candidate sub species (H.erectus or H.heidelbergensis) were brought into the H.sapien family? Who were these giants in the Earth? That's an easy one. Homo heidelbergensis lived between 400,000 and 200,000 years ago. The first H.sapien (legendary Adam) appears in the fossil record about 200 to 300,000 years ago. Homo hcidelbergensis males were on average 2.3 metres (7 feet 6 inches) in height, big enough for an early H.sapien (5 feet 5 inches) to think of as something of a giant.

So there we have it, an interbreeding of sub species of hominins. No great mystery after all, just the time honoured tradition of folks getting it on with the neighbours, nothing new about that then. What is new is the recent discovery by geneticists that H.heidelbergensis was probably the sub species that H.sapiens evolved from, indicating a continuous lineage. Here's the Biblical version again.

Genesis 6:4 ***There were giants in the earth in those days;*** *and also after that, when the sons of God came in unto the daughters of men, and they bare children to them, the same became mighty men* ***which were of old, men of renown.***
So, after Cain found a wife, and presumably had daughters, these giants mated with them, producing kids that grew up

into men like those of old, 'men of renown' (well known). With their father's DNA they grew into big men, the same as their now famous ancestors, H.heidelbergensis.

Most Biblical scholars choose to ignore the fact that there were others of the genus Homo that lived alongside H.sapiens when we first appeared in the fossil record. These scholars don't appear to have the wish to reconcile the science with their dogma. If they did they just might find that a lot more people took their teachings seriously, and that they'd make a lot more sense. They (the scriptures) are, after all, concerned only with us H.s.sapiens, and so there is no great need for them to refer to 'outsiders'.

Fortunately I do not consider myself a scholar, so I have no agenda to promote, and no academic reputation to sustain. I am free to look outside the Christian-Judeo scriptures for answers.

The ancient scriptures were written with us in mind, a sort of user manual. Henry Ford wouldn't put a Mercedes Benz manual in one of his cars, would he? So why should the writers of Genesis mention the others sub species of human? I was once told by an acquaintance that she didn't believe the dinosaurs ever existed. Puzzled by this (to me) outrageous statement, I asked her why she thought this. Her answer was simple and unequivocal.

'They are not mentioned in our Holy Scriptures.'

Very true, apart from 'Leviathan' (probably some sort of whale) in the Old Testament, there is no mention of any creature that could be construed as one of the long extinct reptilians. It doesn't mean they didn't exist though.

<u>A problem with authenticity.</u>

Genesis 4:22 states that Tubal Cane was the forger of instruments of brass and iron. I must point out that Moses was alive in the Bronze Age, a fact which seems to be borne out by Egyptian history. During this period of time, the only iron known to man was meteoric iron, a substance that was considered a gift from the Gods and was extremely rare and valuable. Working it is extremely difficult as it is very brittle, and requires great skill to make anything usable. If Tubal-Cain was a forger of iron, then he would have been considered the equivalent of a nuclear physicist. Men who could work meteoric iron were invariably employed by Kings and as smelted iron was not known in Moses' time, the writer of the Pentateuch either mentioned Tubal-Cain because of his extraordinary metal working abilities, or, more likely, he must have been alive several hundred years later.

All this not only shows a distinct lack of awareness of the time period that this was supposed to happen in, but it also shows that the writer of this particular passage was probably living no earlier than 1,200 years BC, when common iron was first used in the Middle East. This leads me to conclude that this part of Genesis is either fictitious, or it could not have been commissioned by Moses, therefore the first five books of the Bible, though attributed to Moses, were neither written nor commissioned by him.

It's more likely they were named after him in recognition of his prominence in the stories.

In this next chapter I will introduce you to the characters that are generally considered as our very ancient ancestors, some of whom lived alongside us in the not too distant past and 'Mighty Men of Old' they were indeed.

3 MEET CAIN'S WIFE & NEIGHBOURS

In this chapter we say 'Hello' to the guys collectively known as the 'Hominins'. These are the various species of humans that preceded us over the past seven million years (Sorry Archbishop Usher, you were way out!). According to the paleoanthropologists (those who undertake the study of ancient peoples) there were at least three or possibly even four species of Hominin that roamed the planet when we, Homo sapiens, first appeared.

You will see from the chart on page 42, that at the time our H.sapiens ancestors first appeared on Earth, H.neanderthalensis, H.floresiensis, H.erectus and H.heidelbergensis, were already living happily together and quite at home (for many millennia) on Mother Earth.

The co-existence of H.sapiens, (us) with these others of our species is a matter of fact. Fossils, tools, DNA, rock paintings and other artefacts make denial of this cohabitation or the existence of the other Hominins intellectually unacceptable. The proof of this is far too strong, the evidence undeniable. If you disagree, then I'm afraid you're wasting your time reading this book. You would be better off employing your limited time on this Earth by visiting the Smithsonian, or any other Natural History Museum and taking a quick course on the history of Mankind. We need *Thinking Men* for this publication, not blind followers of ancient dogma.

We must bear in mind as we progress herein, that times and dates referred to by archaeologists and by theologians are often very vague, and not accurate by any means. Discrepancies of hundreds or even thousands of years are quite common in these disciplines, and often have very little consequence as the time spans being discussed are measured in hundreds of thousands of years. However, we can only go on what information is to hand and hope that the future will bring more precise detail for us to work with.

Neanderthal Man certainly co-existed with the first modern humans, as his history is seen in the fossil records for some 600,000 years before his kind faded into history somewhere about 24 to 30,000 years ago. Many of us have inherited as much as 4% of our DNA from him, so in reality he actually lives on in the shadows of our genetic makeup.

Homo floresiensis, a resident of the island of Flores in Indonesia, was a very small Hominin (nicknamed 'The Hobbit') who passed out of the fossil record at about the same time, or, if recent discoveries and conjecture are correct, possibly as little as three thousand years ago.

The subject of some discussion about his origins and his period of existence is H.heidelbergensis. He went extinct about 200,000 years ago, just after we came on the scene, although some paleoanthropologists say he had gone before that. Other anthropologists are of the opinion that we had a long period of co-existence with him because recent fossil finds in Morocco suggest we appeared as long ago as 300,000 years. H.heidelbergensis is also considered by some to be our direct evolutionary predecessor. If so, then the inference that Cain married one of them is spot on.

As I said, there is always a margin for error in these dates and many of the experts disagree on the various timescales.

There is also H.erectus, who migrated out of Africa across Asia and parts of Europe one and a half million years ago, and who may have given rise to H. heidelbergensis, but who seems to have outlived him in some parts of the world. He too was probably roaming the Middle East about the same time, and incidentally, was the most successful species of Hominin in terms of time (nearly 2 million years) to have ever lived.

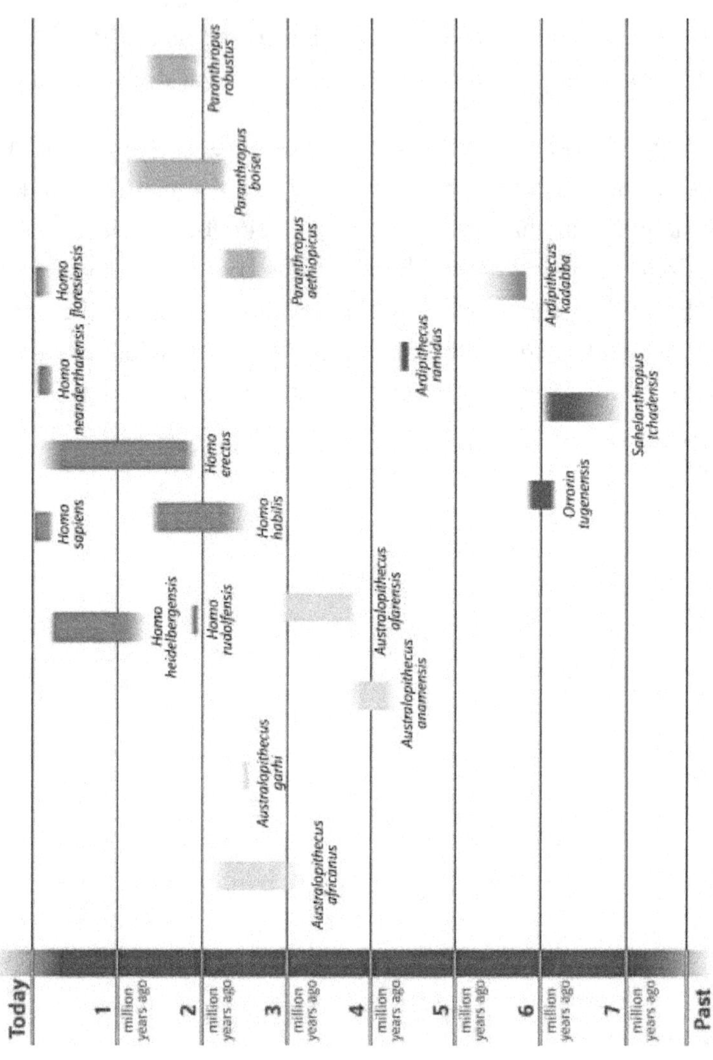

So here we have the fact that, in total, there were four different species of Hominin living at the same time as the original Homo sapiens as we shall have to call them now. This not only avoids confusion, but also prevents us mixing our anthropological metaphors, so to speak. 'Adam and Eve' does not sit well beside 'Homo erectus' etc.

So how do these guys and gals fit in to the Biblical set up? With Human nature being what it is; and make no mistake about it, these other guys were definitely human; a little social intercourse, as well as the other kind, would be quite acceptable.   Granted, the quotation says that Men had begun 'to multiply on the face of the Earth' but who's to say that this statement doesn't include the other sub- species in that particular bit of multiplying?

Why Cain's Wife was H.heidelbergensis

Let's look back at the Biblical reference to there being 'giants in the land' at the time Cain went wife hunting.

H.neanderthalensis (Neanderthal Man) was certainly alive at the same time as H.sapiens. Could it be that Cain found a mate in the population of Neanderthal females?

According to the Max Planck Institute for Evolutionary Anthropology in Leipzig, as much as 4% of Eurasian Homo s.sapien DNA was contributed by Homo Neanderthalensis. Much more robust than us and vastly superior in strength, Neanderthal man would have been a formidable character for a H.sapiens male to face up to, or for a H.sapiens female to say 'no' to. However, at an average height (for an adult male) of 1.64 metres, (or 5 feet 4 inches in Old English) giants **they were not.** What rules him out completely is the fact that H. neanderthalensis never lived in Africa.

H.erectus was probably a stronger individual than H.sapiens, but at between 4 ft. 9 in and 6 ft. 1 in (145 - 185 cm) this guy could hardly be described as a giant, could he?

At about a metre tall, we can safely rule out the 'Hobbit' as a giant mate for Cain, too.

That leaves Homo heidelbergensis. According to the Smithsonian Institute, Human Origins Program, H.heidelbergensis was widespread in Africa and had colonised the Middle East and Asia by 200,000 years ago. Would he fit the description?

H. heidelbergensis are described by paleo archaeologists as being 175 cms in height with females being around 157 cms. (5ft 9 ins and 5ft 2 ins respectively) roughly the same size as us.

However, Professor Lee Berger of the University of Witwatersrand in South Africa is giving us quite a different picture of the early human evolution: He says that numerous fossil bones indicate some populations of Homo Heidelbergensis were "giants", routinely over 2.13 m (7ft) tall and inhabited South Africa between 0.5 million and 300,000 years ago. Some of them were even taller.

At least one archaeologist refutes Berger's claim but he is pictured holding one of these H.heidelbergensis bones in front of normal sized bones - and there is no doubt that it is much larger. Several giant stone tools have also been found in the Kalahari Desert of Africa, and Professor David Thomas of the University of Oxford has confirmed that four of the hand-axes they found were more than 30 centimetres long.

Here are some statistics from the South African population of H heidelbergensis.

Brain capacity: Similar to Homo s.sapien
Upper body strength: Exceeds Homo s.sapien
Average Height: 2.3 metres
Running speed: Exceeds Homo s. s.sapien

With some of these guys nearly eight feet, this species would be much taller than early H.sapien. The females, who after all are not only the subject of this particular hypothesis, but also subject to sexual dimorphism, (difference in size between male and female) would be shorter, probably by some 20-25 per cent, making them about 6 feet, (1.85 metres) but quite acceptable as a mate for our Cain.

Were these 'giants' actually Homo heidelbergensis? Have we found a possible mate for Cain?

We will of course, never know for certain, but the circumstantial evidence is compelling. Sadly, unless the guys working on the DNA extraction and sequencing processes come up with some new findings from the fossilised remains of H.erectus and H.heidelbergensis, we will never know, but I suspect I will be proved right.

What about the other, 'mystical' beings?

Apart from the Giants, the 1st Book of Enoch tells us of sightings of other beings. This book of the Apocrypha was written about 2nd–1st century BC and is based on one interpretation of the 'Sons of God' (the Giants) passage in Genesis 6, according to which interpretation, angels consorted with human females, giving rise to a race of hybrids known as the Nephilim. However, the is no mention of females in this population of Nephilim, and so I think we can rule them out as candidates for Cain's wife, although it is possible that one of their human wives may have had a daughter. Given the physical evidence supporting the existence of H.heidelbergensis, and the lack of it for the Nephilim, I'm going to come down in favour of H. heidelbergensis.

Some Biblical scholars say the Nephilim were the 'Grigori', or the 'Watchers' sent from Heaven to keep an eye on mankind and report back to God on the progress or otherwise being made by humans.

These guys were angels who, according to the scholars, being all male, eventually were tempted by, and succumbed to, the sexual charms of human females. They were eventually rounded up and chained together and cast into a deep pit.

The term **Irin** is primarily applied to the promiscuous Watchers who numbered a total of 200, but equally in Aramaic **iri** ("watcher" singular) is also applied to the obedient archangels who chained the naughty ones together, such as Raphael (1 Enoch 22:6).

All well and good, but not really in keeping with the theological theme of the Good Book is it? Surely the Angels are pure creatures, above such depravity and the temptations of the flesh, and since when have the beings of Heaven 'got it on' with the flesh and blood of Earth? As far as I know, apart from Mary (the mother of Jesus) and possibly Sarah (the mother of Ishmael), it never happened. Would the citizens of Heaven be sexual creatures anyway? What need for sexuality in immortal creatures created by God?

 So it seems a little suspect, do you not think, or at the very least, out of the ordinary? In any case, there don't seem to have been many confirmed reports of angels frequenting modern society, let alone doing the business with us Earthlings. On the other hand, it could be that the often reported alien abductions are not quite what the victims' claim. It seems to me that something a little more straightforward, and if you'll excuse the pun, more down to earth, would be the explanation.

I can once again envisage a rather baffled scribe trying to make sense of the old folk tales about giants and strange sounding non-human people. He would be sitting there chewing his quill and thinking that these must be some sort of divine beings (the Bronze Age equivalent of an extra-terrestrial) that are being described. Little did he know that the stories could be taken at face value. It would never have occurred to him that there was once more than one type of human.

Drawing together the religious legend and the known facts may seem to some of you a ridiculous, even preposterous thing to do, but the similarities are there, and they cannot be ignored if we are to unearth the truth about our past and our written legends. Remember to keep an open mind and think about ALL the possibilities. As the Bible is in effect a history of mankind, why should we be surprised to find that it gives us provable information? If you are scientifically minded, then truth is your stock in trade. If you are religiously minded then the reality of this world is God's doing. Either way, if it's actually a true fact, it can't be proven to be otherwise.

The characters we have referred to as Adam and Eve, and Cain and Able, represent, to me at least, not an individual person, but a whole family, the newly arisen family of H.sapiens. The killing of Able would appear to be a symbolic act accounting for the (apparent) demise of the other sub species.

It has been proven that interbreeding with the other species took place and it probably gave us the anatomical capabilities and intellectual abilities that we are blessed with. A small genetic mutation at the same time would be quite sufficient to send us off on the path to independence as a separate species, leaving behind the 'giants in the land' and dominating the world.

5 CO-ORDINATES OF THE GARDEN OF EDEN

Everybody lives somewhere. Most of us describe ourselves by our geographical origins. I, for example would describe myself as an Englishman. If I was in conversation with another Englishman, I would say I was a Yorkshire man. This method of self-description is pretty common around the world. We all relate to the place where we were born. Even if, as in my case, we have not actually lived there for decades.

The geographical situation for the legendary Adam, Eve and Cain is somewhat vague by comparison to my own rather mundane origins, even though there is a Land of Nod (Genesis 4:16) just a few miles from my birth place in East Yorkshire. As beautiful as Yorkshire is, I somehow don't see it as the site of the Garden of Eden.

For centuries people have been trying to work out where the original couple described in Genesis lived. No doubt an idea is in their heads that by going to this place, they will be nearer to God, or at least, at the very centre of the Human Universe. I don't deny that I would be just as keen as anyone else to visit, if it could be proved where The Garden of Eden actually used to be. However, I suspect that my motives would be a little different to the majority of Eden tourists.

So where was it, this Paradise on Earth? If indeed it actually was on Earth. Shall we peruse the evidence and see what can be made of it? It's been done hundreds of times before, and never with any real success, but let's have a go anyway. I'm feeling lucky today.

There are some accounts of Adam and Eve 'falling to Earth' after they were expelled from the Garden, but the biblical accounts infer that their paradise was actually here on Earth. Islamic tradition says that the Ka'ba, the central building in the Great Mosque in Mecca, was built upon the place where Adam and Eve 'fell to Earth', but it is more likely that the old legends identify this area as the place where modern man began his colonisation of the planet after leaving Africa.

Scholars generally describe the Garden of Eden as lying somewhere between the Horn of African and Turkey, and between the River Nile and the Persian Gulf. There is in this passage from the Bible, a definitive description of the whereabouts of the Garden of Eden.

Holy Bible (King James Version) Genesis 2:10-15

2:10 And a river went out of Eden to water the garden; and from thence it was parted, and became into four heads.

2:11 The name of the first is Pison: that is it which compasseth the whole land of Havilah, where there is gold;

2:12 And the gold of that land is good: there is bdellium and the onyx stone.

2:13 And the name of the second river is Gihon: the same is it that compasseth the whole land of Ethiopia.

2:14 And the name of the third river is Hiddekel: that is it which goeth toward the east of Assyria. And the fourth river is Euphrates.

2:15 And the LORD God took the man, and put him into the garden of Eden to dress it and to keep it.

Existing Theories

Shall we consider the merits of the other theories that have been put forward? So what have we got then? Let's list the Biblical clues.

Eden, a Babylonian name meaning 'plain'.

A Garden, lying eastward in Eden

A River, unnamed, coming out of Eden, through the garden

Pison, a river head linked with Havilah

Havilah, a land or district

Gihon, a river linked with Ethiopia

Ethiopia, Cush (in Hebrew); a land or district

Hiddekel, a river linked with Assyria

Assyria, (Asshur in Hebrew); not called "a land"

Euphrates, a river existing today.

A Flaming Sword to the East

First, we know that the river Euphrates runs through Turkey into Iraq. That's for sure, I can personally attest to its existence. So the first river is sorted.

Secondly, we should look at the Hiddekel. It is also fairly easy to identify. Whilst not everyone reading English will immediately recognize the name "Hiddekel', scholars are quite in agreement about it. It is the modern Tigris. The ancient Sumerians called the Tigris, "Idikna" or "Idikla." The early Semitic people called it, "Idiklat" (in Hebrew,"Hiddekel,"), later shortened to "Diklat." The Persians pronounced it, "Tigra," from whence the classical Greek name came, "Tigris." Today, in Arabic it is, "Dijla." Once again, these are but variants of one name retained throughout all history. This identification is upon firm ground. To make the identification doubly sure, the Tigris is definitely the river of Assyria. The Assyrian capital city Nineveh stood upon that river's banks.

The other two, however, are not so easy to identify. Pison (2:11) is said here to 'compass' the whole land of Havilah, where the gold is. What comes to mind when we think about the ancient world and gold? How about the ancient Egyptians? Their gold was mined in what was, and by some people is still known as, Nubia, or Upper Egypt, through which, for thousands of years, has, of course, run the Nile. The Nile would be a very suitable contender for the Pison. However, Arabia was also famous for gold and there is the reference to 'bdellium and the onyx stone' Bdellium is generally thought to be an aromatic gum like myrrh that is exuded from a tree, which brings to mind the incense produced in the south of the Arabian Peninsula. There is here, the dried out river known as Wadi Bisha, (phonetically very close to 'Pison') which begins in the Hijaz Mountains near Medina to run northeast to Kuwait. This would make another good contender for the title of Pison.

In 1995, James Sauer, the former curator of the Harvard Semitic Museum, made an argument from geology and history that 'Pison' referred to the Wadi Bisha. David Rohl, Co-Field Director of the Eastern Desert Survey in Egypt, identified Pison with the Uizhun, placing Havilah to the northeast of Mesopotamia. The Uizhun is known locally in Iran as the Golden River. Rising near Mount Sahand, it meanders between ancient gold mines and lodes of lapis lazuli before feeding the Caspian Sea. Such natural resources correspond to the ones associated with the land of Havilah in Genesis 2:11.

Next we have the Gihon. There is much evidence as to which river this is or was. The first-century Jewish historian, Josephus associated the Gihon river with the Nile (Jewish Antiquities, 1.39), the name (Hebrew: Giħôn) may be interpreted as "Bursting Forth, Gushing". As such, it is identified as the Karkheh, that along with the Karun, share their deltaic marshlands with the Tigris and Euphrates in the Sumerian edin/Eden to the present day.

The Gihon is also described as "encircling the entire land of Cush", a name associated with Ethiopia elsewhere in the Bible. This is one of the reasons that Ethiopians have long identified the Gihon with the Abay River, which encircles the former Horn of Africa kingdom of Gojjam.

It's at this point that the whole thing becomes, from a current geographic standpoint, impossible, since two of the other rivers said to issue out of Eden, the Tigris and the Euphrates, are in Mesopotamia (Iraq).

Some nineteenth century, modern, and Arabic scholars have sought to identify the "land of Cush" with Hindu Kush, and Gihon with Amu Darya (Jihon/Jayhon of the Islamic texts). The Amu Darya was known by the medieval Islamic writers as Jayhun (Ceyhun in Turkish). This was a derivative of Jihon, or Zhihon as it is still known by the Persians.

We must bear in mind that way back in time, people lived in tribes, and each tribe had a name. Accordingly, if you went to visit, you went to the Land of the Smiths, or whatever. As a consequence, areas became associated with tribes, and if the tribe moved, then the place name moved too. So, the Land of the Cush may well have been several different places over time. All very vague when it comes to positive identification.

It is interesting to note that in Ethiopia, there are Jewish communities (known as Beta Israel and recognised by Israel) that claim Ethiopia is the 'Land of Cush'. Beta Israel live in North and North-Western Ethiopia in more than 500 small villages spread over a wide territory, among Muslim and predominantly Christian ruling populations. So a Hebrew connection with Ethiopia is established, but not necessarily making Ethiopia a candidate for Eden.

But are these rivers actually the boundaries of The Garden?

It's here we come face to face with the 'Elephant in the Room'. We cannot ignore the fact that Ethiopia and the surrounding area is the site of many of the earliest known Hominin fossil finds. This alone must make it a serious contender for the site of the 'Garden of Eden'. Gihon has also been associated with the Araxes (modern Aras) river of Armenia. However, another proposed idea is that the Gihon River no longer exists, or has significantly altered its course, since the topography of the area has supposedly been altered by Noah's Flood.

It Is a theory that has some validity. This whole area is shaped and influenced by the movement of the African and Arabian plates as they squeeze Turkey against the Eurasian plate. Some scholars argue that the Gihon river remains unidentified since the geographical ideas of the author of Genesis cannot be reconstructed and need not conform to actual geography as known. The problem is of course, that even the whole 2-300,000 years of Human existence is a very short time span in geological terms. Even so, let me illustrate just how much and how (relatively) quickly geography can change.

Iceland is one of the most geologically active places on Earth. In the past 10,000 years the Thingvellir Rift Valley has been drastically changed in appearance by the spreading and sinking of the Earth's crust and by earthquakes. Measurements suggest that the floor of the valley has widened 230 feet (70 m) and sunk by 131 feet (40

m) in the space of 10,000 years. Iceland is one of the most geologically active places on Earth with more than 15 volcanoes that have erupted in the last century.

North of the Arabian Peninsula, the 'Holy Land' is affected by the African 'Great Rift Valley', which extends through the Red Sea and along the Jordan Valley. It is, geologically speaking, very dynamic, but very much less so than Iceland. There hasn't been a volcanic eruption in the 'Holy Land' region for tens of thousands of years. The Dead Sea owes its very existence to this huge fault line, sinking over time to become the lowest place on earth.

And now for something completely different....

Gobekli Tepe

There is another candidate for the Garden, and its qualifications are impressive, to say the least.

A Kurdish shepherd was tending his sheep on the plains of eastern Turkey. Following his flock over the hillsides, he passed the single mulberry tree which the locals have long regarded as 'sacred'. No one quite knew why it was sacred, but sacred it was. He saw a large flat stone. Crouching down, he brushed away the dust, and exposed a strange, large, oblong stone. The man looked left and right: there were similar stone rectangles buried in the ground nearby. He decided to tell someone about his find when he got back to the village. Maybe the stones were important? They certainly were.

That solitary Kurdish man, on that summer's day in 1994, had made what some say is the greatest archaeological discovery in 50 years. Others say he'd made the greatest archaeological discovery ever: a site that has revolutionised the way we look at human history and the origin of religion.

He had found Gobekli Tepe, the oldest Temple in the world. Its age is staggering. Carbon-dating shows that the complex is at least 10,000 years old, maybe even 12,000 years old. If indeed Gobekli Tepi was built 10-12,000 years ago it was built around 10,000BC. By comparison, Stonehenge was built in 3,000 BC and the pyramids of Giza in 2,500 BC. If you visit the area, or even if you just read up on it, you will very quickly realise that several unique factors lift Gobekli Tepe into the realms of the fantastic.

Gobekli is the oldest such site in the world, by a mind-numbing margin. It is so old that it predates settled human life. It is pre-pottery, pre-writing, pre-everything. Gobekli hails from a part of human history that is unimaginably distant in terms of the history of civilisation: right back in our hunter-gatherer past. It pre dates mankind's (presumed) ability to build it. Certainly it predates any other stone building by many centuries.

This region's history is writ large in the Bible. Gobekli Tepe is just a few kilometres from a city called Sanliurfa (or 'Urfa to the locals). The history of Sanliurfa is recorded from the 4th century BC, but may date back to 8000 BC. It was one of several cities in the Euphrates-Tigris basin, the cradle of the Mesopotamian civilization. According to Turkish Muslim traditions, Urfa (its name since Byzantine days) is the Biblical city of Ur because of its proximity to the village of Haran. Genesis 27:43 makes Haran the home of Laban and connects it with Isaac and Jacob: it was the home of Isaac's wife Rebekah, and their son Jacob spent twenty years in Haran working for his uncle Laban (Genesis 31:38 & 41).

Urfa is said by the locals to be the birthplace of Abraham, although the vast majority of scholars agree that Ur, the city in Northern Iraq, is the place where the Patriarch was born. Urfa is also known as the birthplace of Job, who incidentally, is buried not very far away in a small hamlet called Ayupp Nabi, (means, Job the Prophet) where you will find, all within 100 metres, the grave of Job's wife and the prophet Elijah, who was Job's friend. The tombs are the site of pilgrimage and have been faithfully tended by the Gifty family for many generations. Whilst it is not a known tourist spot due to the political tensions there, it is well worth a visit, if only to connect with the biblical characters.

The Book of Genesis says that Eden is west of Assyria. Sure enough, this is where Gobekli is. Likewise, it says that Eden is bounded by four rivers, including the Tigris and Euphrates, and Gobekli lies between both of these.

In ancient Assyrian texts, there is mention of a 'Beth Eden' - a house of Eden. This minor kingdom was 50 miles from Gobekli Tepe. The Second Book of Kings refers to 'the children of Eden which were in Thelasar', a town in northern Syria, near Gobekli.

Holy Bible (King James Version) 2 Kings 19:11-12

19:11 Behold, thou hast heard what the kings of Assyria have done to all lands, by destroying them utterly: and shalt thou be delivered?

19:12 Have the gods of the nations delivered them **which my fathers have destroyed; as Gozan, and Haran, and Rezeph, and the children of Eden which were in Thelasar?**

Now there's a thing. Apparently the 'Children of Eden' have been destroyed! Are we looking at a scenario where the other species of Hominin are considered to be the Original People? Is the population of Homo s.sapien an occupying invader who has destroyed and replaced those to whom the Book of Genesis refers? Have we as a race hijacked the scriptures of another older population? Do the ancient Scriptures not belong or apply to us? We have certainly replaced other populations, of that there is no doubt.

The very word 'Eden' comes from the Sumerian for 'plain'; Gobekli lies on the plains of Haran. So, when you put it all together, the evidence is persuasive. Gobekli Tepe is, indeed, a 'temple in Eden', built by our distant ancestors, people who had time to cultivate art, architecture and complex ritual, before agriculture ruined their lifestyle, and devastated their paradise.

Curiously, the loss of their paradise seems to have had a strange and darkening effect on the occupants of Gobekli Tepe. The very people who worshipped at this ancient temple, buried it deliberately to hide it. This was a massive undertaking and no one knows for sure why they did it, but it has been suggested that they were so devastated by the loss of their hunter gather lifestyle, that they hid the place from view so as not to be reminded of 'the good old days'!

The Persian Gulf

So why does it matter? And does it matters that it matters? Is it really so important to pinpoint The Garden of Eden? As an academic point, it is of more interest to those interested in past cultures and theology than it is to those who are seeking the origin of the human species. Biblical stories are usually based on some truth, as are all good legends. It is all rather vague, but based on the evidence and the logical arguments presented, as a 'second best' theory, the argument that the legendary Land of Eden, and it's Garden, would have been situated somewhere around the head of the Persian Gulf is compelling. Here's why.

Several thousand years ago, when sea levels were lower, the area at the head of the Persian Gulf was lush and well-watered. It was not until the melting of the ice between 110,000 and 10,000 years ago that the Persian Gulf was formed by the rise in global sea levels. This area almost fits the Genesis description, and there are many folk tales that point to it as the place where many peoples originated. Several scholars also indicate this general region as being the most likely area indicated in the scriptures. The Ka'ba, in the Great Mosque in Mecca, situated to the South West of this area is said to be built at the place where Adam and Eve were expelled from the Garden. Again, is it possible that this describes the exit by H.sapiens from Africa?

<u>Enough of the speculation and wild guesses and Bronze Age hypothesising. Let's get logical.</u>

It's time to study the atlas. The description of the river that runs out of Eden and <u>divides</u> into four heads brings to my mind the Okavango Delta.

Co-ordinates are: 19.6510° S, 22.9059° E

The Okavango River rises in Angola and runs into Botswana. Here, just like the description in Genesis, the river splits into four and each individual water course runs until it finally gives up the fight and evaporates into extinction. It's the world's largest inland delta. It's formed where the Okavango River empties onto a swamp in a basin in the Kalahari Desert, and the water is lost to evaporation instead of draining into the sea. Each year approximately 11 cubic kilometres of water irrigate the 15,000 km² area. During the period when this region is flooded, it teems with life; from the tiniest birds to the mightiest Elephants, truly a haven for life in the middle of the desert.

This area was once part of Lake Makgadikgadi, an ancient lake that dried up by the early Holocene, about 10,000 years ago. The Delta's greenery is not the result of a tropical climate; it's an oasis in the Kalahari Desert. Annual rainfall is about 450mm, most of it falling between December and March in the form of heavy afternoon thunderstorms. December to February are hot wet months with daytime temperatures as high as 40°C, with warm nights. From

March to May the temperature becomes far more comfortable with a maximum of 30°C during the day and mild to cool nights. The rains quickly dry up leading into the dry, cold winter months of June to August. Daytime temperatures at this time of year are mild to warm but the temperature begins to fall after sunset. These conditions would make it a very hospitable environment indeed for a newly emerged Hominin species.

It fits the description that the account in Genesis gives very well, except of course that it is a very long way from the one river named in Genesis 3 verses 23-24 that we can readily identify, the Euphrates.

Looking at the other clues in Genesis, we see that Botswana has a thriving diamond industry, and there's no doubt there is gold hereabouts; Botswana produces about 1000 ounces of the stuff annually and there is the famous Black Onyx of Botswana. No one knows for sure what Bdellium is, or was, but if any place on Earth would have it, I'm sure that mineral rich and florally diverse Africa could come up with some.

There are other considerations that must be taken into account when discussing this issue. It isn't just the Bible that holds clues as to our origins. The findings by The Study of African Genetic Diversity, headed by Dr. Sarah Tishkoff, of the University of Pennsylvania, for instance, has located the origin of modern human migration (the Out of Africa migration, not the Mediterranean one in rubber boats) in south-western Africa, near the border of Namibia and Angola.

Another group of researchers say they've pinpointed the ancestral homeland of all humans alive today: modern-day Botswana. In a 2019 study published in the journal Nature, scientists analysed mitochondrial DNA (genetic information that only gets passed down the female line) from more than 1,200 people across myriad populations in Africa. By examining which genes were preserved in people's DNA over time, the anthropologists determined that anatomically modern humans emerged in what was once a lush wetland in Botswana, south of the Zambezi River. Anthropologist Vanessa Hayes, the senior author of the paper said in a press conference that the findings suggest "everyone walking around today" can trace their mitochondrial DNA back to this "human homeland."

The Okavango Delta lies on the borders of Angola, Namibia in Botswana, just south of the Zambezi river, in the Kalahari Desert. The Okavango and the Zambezi rivers would make a natural transition route from here, across Africa. Migrants would follow them to utilize the water as they transited the region to arrive in the savannahs of East Africa, the site of so many old human fossil finds.

All that is needed to complete the picture is a flaming sword to the East. Well, the African Rift Valley and the East of Africa have many volcanos; how about one of these for a 'flaming sword'? If volcanos don't appeal to your idea of a 'flaming sword', how about the burning Kalahari desert itself? Deserts have always been natural barriers to both animals and mankind, so this particular desert would easily 'keep the way' to the Okavango Garden.

It all seems to fit the general description of the legend much better than the present consensus putting the Garden of Eden in the Iran/Iraq region. I know that all the experts will probably point and laugh, but I can't help thinking about all the ancient fossils of Hominins discovered in East Africa, right across from the Okavango region. If we connect all the evidence it gives us our earliest humans in a well-watered garden on a plain, with four river heads and with a 'flaming sword' just to the east.

There is of course the discrepancy in the time frame for the Okavango Delta and the rise of H.sapiens. Whilst the earliest H.sapiens lived almost 200-300,000 years ago when Lake Makgadikgadi dominated the area prior to the Delta coming into existence, it must be noted that the *location* is the same. This large freshwater lake in the middle of the desert would have been (and the Delta still is) a focal point for all life in the region.

The Delta would be an ideal landmark for those trying to describe where to find the area. For example, if I were to try and describe to you where the excavated Viking village called the Viking Centre in York, England is, I would tell you it is in Coppergate, next to the Coppergate Shopping Mall opposite the Norman church. This description wouldn't lead you to think that the shopping mall or the church existed at the same time as the Vikings or the Norman's lived in York, but in our time context it would provide a description of the area that would enable you to find it.

As for naming the rivers of the Garden, if the writers of Genesis had not known for sure the names of the rivers referred to in the ancient folk tales that they were transcribing they may well have named the ones they did know. These rivers all bear vague similarities to the Okavango Delta which they would not have known about. To them it would all make sense. We'll never know for sure, of course, but it bears consideration wouldn't you say? After all, they tell me that writers always take a few liberties with reality. I mean of course, the writers of Genesis, not yours truly.

The Okavangavango Delta within the Kalahari Desert

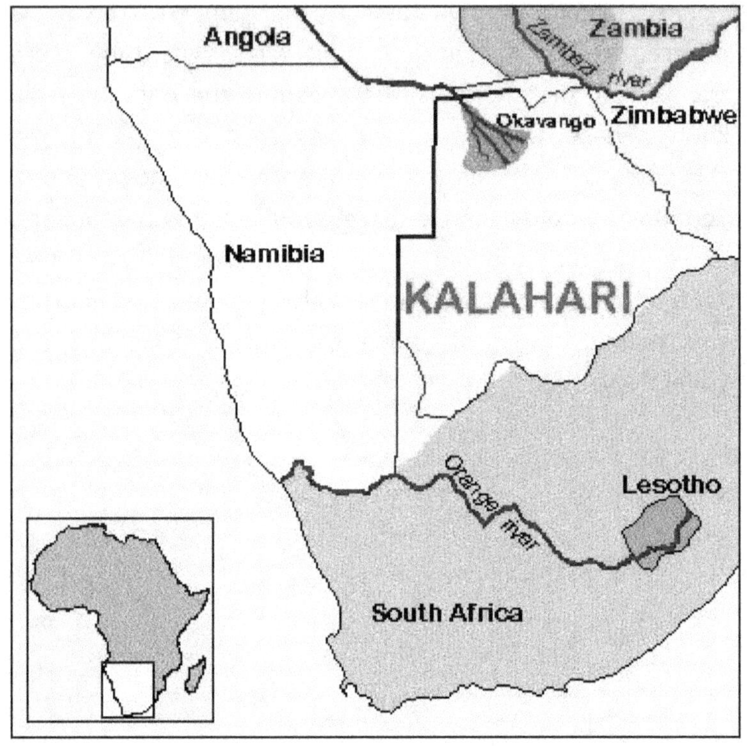

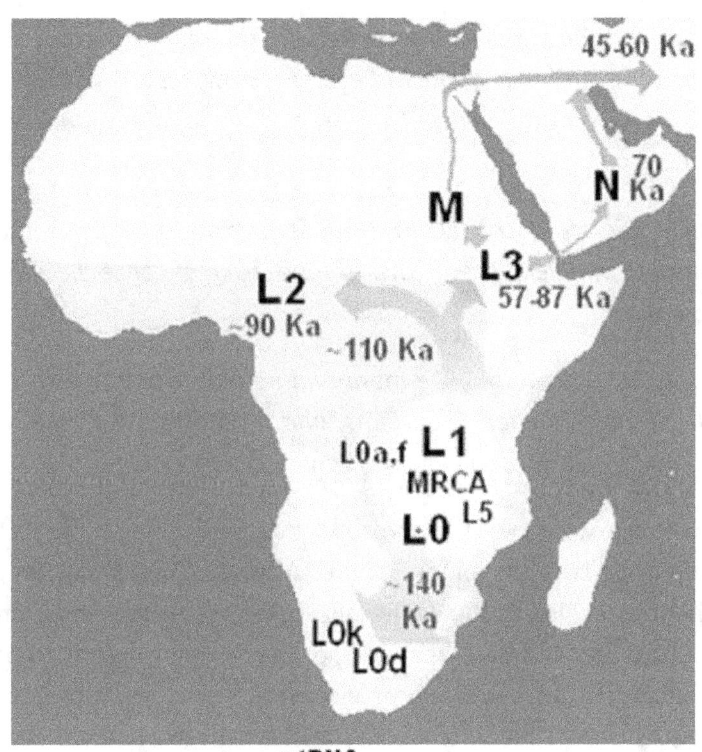
45-60 Ka
N 70 Ka
M
L3
57-87 Ka
L2
~90 Ka
~110 Ka
L0a,f L1
MRCA
L0 L5
~140 Ka
L0k
L0d

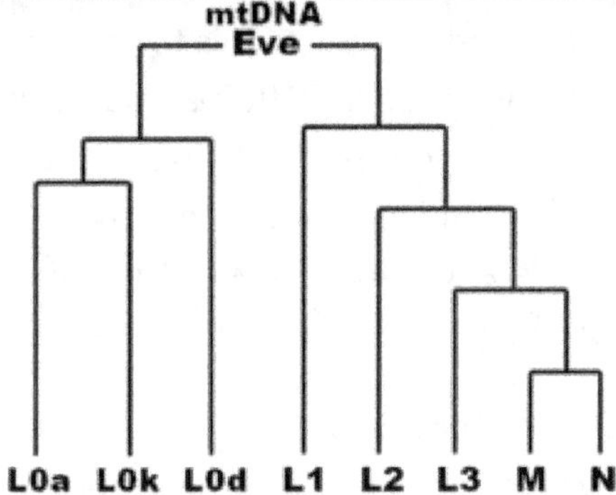
mtDNA
Eve
L0a L0k L0d L1 L2 L3 M N

Holy Bible (King James Version) Genesis 3:22-24

3:22 And the LORD God said, Behold, the man is become as one of us, to know good and evil: and now, lest he put forth his hand, and take also of the tree of life, and eat, and live for ever:

3:23 Therefore the LORD God sent him forth from the garden of Eden, to till the ground from whence he was taken.

3:24 So he drove out the man; and he placed at the east of the garden of Eden Cherubims, and a flaming sword which turned every way, to keep the way of the tree of life.

So there we have it. Adam and Eve leave the Garden of Eden. Or is it H.sapiens leaving Africa? This is the only theory (at least the only one I've seen) that has an explanation, if only a weak one, of the 'Flaming Sword'; that matches the archaeological discoveries; and fits the DNA sequencing. The Delta even matches the story that Cain 'went East to the Land of Nod' as it is to the West of the site of the earliest known Human DNA (see map of mDNA). How much more proof do you need? Come to that, what other proof exists that could be furnished? The other theories ignore the reference to other Hominins and just concentrate on the rivers mentioned.

All my facts fit, and they fit better than any other theory. In fact, I'd be willing to wager a month's beer money that most paleoanthropologists would prefer my theory to any other.

All we have to go on is an ancient folk memory written down nearly four thousand years ago about events that seem to have occurred about 165,000 years earlier (see: Clothes Maketh Man). So I won't apologise for this theory being well off the track beaten by others. The writers of Genesis may well have been as much in the dark about the location of the Garden of Eden as we are, so they made an educated guess as to the names of the rivers, applying their own (limited) local knowledge.

The 'Out of Africa' theory describes the expansion of H.sapiens as a race, into the world outside of its original homeland. It says that we crossed the Red Sea's Bab el Mandab at the southern tip of Arabia, and followed the coast line to India, with a branch of intrepid colonists working their way up the Persian Gulf shore. Genesis seems to take up the story from there. Those early colonisers took their folk tales with them.

The Garden of Eden can also be viewed symbolically. A paradise where all you need is available just by picking it up. This is an idea not far removed from the somewhat more difficult life of the hunter gatherer. When the farming community settled in the plains of the Fertile Triangle, tilling the soils and displacing both the migrating animals and the hunters, the good old days were gone for ever. The hunter was literally forced from his paradise, his Garden of Eden, the Garden on the Plain (of Central Africa?) by the advance of agriculture. Folk memories often recall such changes in society, the stories becoming more and more elaborate as one story teller after another adds his own embellishment.

This 'Agricultural Revolution' marked a turning point for Mankind. From that point in time we were doomed to extinction. We had abandoned the natural ways and were to pay the price in over population, disease, and eventually, by way of industrial development, to climate change and the destruction of our habitat and ourselves.

More to the point, and much less controversial to any school of thought other than my own, is the fact that the Middle East is most definitely the *starting point*, or at least a *transition point*, of H.sapiens journey to world domination. Whether you follow the religious or scientific theories, the Middle East conforms both to Genesis and the Out of Africa theories in this respect. Whether it was actually the *birthplace* of H.sapien is not in doubt. That was definitely inside the African continent......

......in the Okavango Delta 'Garden of Eden', right where mDNA sequencing shows the first humans arose and where H.heidelbergensis used to be the 'giant in the land'.

Q.E.D.[57]

You don't agree with my theory? I'm willing to listen to criticisms, of which I expect many.

I'm an easy going guy. Just because I'm right doesn't mean I'll hold a grudge....

6 VIRUM VESTIS FACIT - CLOTHES MAKETH MAN

So the new inhabitants of Earth, have arrived, ex. Paradise. Just to rub it in and make Bishop Usher even more embarrassed, we can probably date the occurrence mentioned in this next chapter of Genesis to approximately 170,000 years ago. Just how we can do it, is definitely beyond good taste and well and truly in the realm of the scientist.

Holy Bible (King James Version) Genesis 3:20 – 24

3:20 And Adam called his wife's name Eve; because she was the mother of all living.

3:21 Unto Adam also and to his wife did the LORD God make coats of skins, and clothed them.

3:22 And the LORD God said, Behold, the man is become as one of us, to know good and evil: and now, lest he put forth his hand, and take also of the tree of life, and eat, and live for ever:

3:23 Therefore the LORD God sent him forth from the garden of Eden, to till the ground from whence he was taken.

3:24 So he drove out the man; and he placed at the east of the garden of Eden Cherubims, and a flaming sword which turned every way, to keep the way of the tree of life.

Now, there are many amazing discoveries in our history that have been made in the most extraordinary circumstances and in the most improbable research, but this next one must surely take the Oscar.

What do you know about lice; head lice, body lice, or pubic lice? Hopefully you have no idea what they look like or feel like. Many people are disgusted even by the very mention of them, but the inescapable fact is that lice have been with us ever since the dawn of our Hominin species. Back then we were covered in hair, so our lice were comfortable on any particular part of our anatomy.

With the arrival of Homo erectus, who began to lose his body hair, the louse found that it now had to specialise. Either as a head louse at, shall we say, the Northern end of his world, or as a pubic hair louse at the Southern end. Body hair had all but disappeared so it was no longer possible to live just anywhere on a convenient human. The louse had to choose. This state of affairs existed for quite some time, about a million years actually, until another option became available. We started wearing clothes and the lice got a third option.

.A University of Florida study following the evolution of human body lice, (I kid you not) proposes modern humans started wearing clothes about 170,000 years ago, a technology which enabled them to successfully migrate out of Africa. Principal investigator David Reed, associate curator of mammals at the Florida Museum of Natural History on the Florida campus, studies lice in modern humans to better understand human evolution and migration patterns. His latest five-year study used DNA sequencing to calculate when clothing lice first began to diverge genetically from human head lice.

"We wanted to find another method for pinpointing when humans might have first started wearing clothing," Reed said. *"Because they are so well adapted to clothing, we know that body lice or clothing lice almost certainly didn't exist until clothing came about in humans."*

The data shows modern humans started wearing clothes about 70,000 years before migrating into colder climates and higher latitudes, which began about 100,000 years ago. This would be impossible to determine using archaeological data because clothing just doesn't survive when it's buried in the ground. As a consequence, it rarely shows up at archaeological digs. The study also shows humans started wearing clothes well after they lost their body hair, which genetic skin-coloration research pinpoints at about 1 million years ago, meaning, Reed says, that humans spent a considerable amount of time without body hair and without clothing.

"It's interesting to think humans were able to survive in Africa for hundreds of thousands of years without clothing and without body hair, and that it wasn't until they had clothing that modern humans were then moving out of Africa into other parts of the world."

Whilst this is an interesting and fairly logical theory, it must be pointed out that according to widespread archaeological evidence, H.erectus migrated out of Africa about 1.0 million years before H.sapiens, colonising the Middle East parts of Europe and Asia. Is David Reed suggesting that H.erectus also wore clothes to enable him to exist in the more hostile environment of the North? That being the case, then surely Humans started wearing clothes long before the time Reed says. About 1.0 million years before. Or did Homo erectus go naked and freeze? I thought only monkeys had brass ones[12], but according to Dr. Reed, H.erectus did too....

The Fur Coat

None of us, or should I say, most of us, are not completely covered in hair, or in its denser form, fur. It's true that some individuals are extremely hairy, but even in the most extreme cases you couldn't say they were furry. Other primates, such as chimps and gorillas, have thick hair all over their bodies. So why do we not have? It's obvious that we need some form of protection from the environment that we live in, outside of Central Africa, so why has body hair been banished from our physiology? I put this very question to the guys I thought most likely to know the answer, the Smithsonian Institute's Human Origin's Program. Their reply was, to say the least, somewhat short of detail, but I thank them for responding to my query.

To: Smithsonian Institute Human Origins Program

Subject: No Fur Coat

Can you explain, or guess, why early humans are depicted as having no fur/body hair? No other primates (that I can recall) are naked. Even in the hottest of climates they have

OK. But Chimps, Gorillas etc., all have thick fur and live in hot climates. They manage to cool their bodies without any problem or hair loss. Why are we different? Admittedly we are (arguably) far more advanced than they are, but what does the lack of hair have to do with it? Evolution theory dictates it must be necessary. Why then, does the fastest animal on the planet, the Cheetah, have a dense fur coat, and cool itself by panting? Surely evolution got it right for him?

Well, it did, but H.erectus was in a different league. Unable to compete with faster predators, or come to that, even catch prey animals, he did what the human species always does. He thought about the problem and came up with a winning fix. The explanation by the Smithsonian cites Homo erectus as probably being the first species to lose hair and develop sweat glands to cool his body. Homo erectus began his dynasty in East Africa about 2 million years ago. The theory runs (if you'll pardon the pun) like this. He had to live on a savannah and had to move quickly between the sparse tree cover to avoid predators, thus evolving a cooling system for his more streamlined, faster running body.

Slower, uncooled body=eaten=no evolution.

Faster, cooled body=escape=live to breed another day.

It may be worth noting that anyone can ask the Smithsonian questions about our origins, and they seem pleased to help. Just e mail them at: ***humanorigins@si.edu***

These early Hominins stood about 1.79 m (5 feet 10 inches), and were more robust than modern humans. The sexual dimorphism (difference in size between the sexes) of males and females was slightly greater than seen in H.sapiens, with males being about 25% larger than females.

The discovery of the skeleton of 'Turkana Boy' made near Lake Turkana, Kenya, by Richard Leakey and Kamoya Kimeu in 1984, is one of the most complete H.ergaster (another extinct close relative) skeletons ever discovered, and has contributed greatly to our understanding of human physical evolution. Turkana Boy had noticeably long legs. He was no 'knuckle dragger' either. Standing tall and straight, he developed a talent that may seem very hard to believe.

He became a long distance runner; a long distance runner of Olympic standards. In fact the *average* H.ergaster could probably put today's champions to shame. He could out run almost any animal on the planet. Not over shorter sprints, but he could give chase to, and eventually run down and kill anything he hunted. That bum of yours is not just for sitting on. Those muscles can power your legs for hours at a time, over huge distances. However, running for extended periods of time quickly causes the body to over-heat, so a furless body would be a huge advantage and necessary to facilitate cooling.

That is a much more complete explanation of why we are furless, don't you think?

H.erectus had tools, had fire, and was quite capable of stitching together animal skins to make effective clothing. Whilst he may not have needed it to protect him from the weather in his original homelands, it would be extremely useful in other areas after he migrated out of Africa.

H.erectus would only have to venture onto the Ararat Mountains in south eastern Turkey, or the Atlas mountains in Morocco to find snow and sub-zero temperatures. Even in Israel winter weather can fluctuate. Some winters are mild and sunny, some severe and overcast. There's often heavy rain and, in January and February, even snow in some parts of the country. It can be cold enough to die from exposure. A fire and clothing would be a must. Any animal native to the area would have fur and have evolved to live there despite the harsh weather.

We've only mentioned the Middle East here, and yet H.erectus fossils have been found as far afield as Morocco and China. There was plenty of extremely cold weather for him to contend with and a huge variation in environments. As David Reed says, clothing would be essential in the absence of a fur covered body.

H.sapiens, venturing out of the comfortable climate of Africa, about 1.0 million years later, would definitely find a need for clothing, and if he did not invent it anew, could have copied, or even traded or stolen it from H.erectus. Given that their African ancestors co-existed, I would suggest that a common use of clothing would have been the case.

H.erectus' average (male) height was a little under six feet, he had a brain capacity almost equal to ours; was considerably stronger and faster than us; migrated out of Africa before us, and yet he still went extinct. Better equipped than us, but he still didn't make it. I wonder why?

Stay tuned to this channel......

How closely did H.erectus and H.sapien co-exist? Did we steal his clothes? Did we catch his, or maybe *her* lice and if we did, that would imply a rather intimate relationship, don't you think?

Which would have suited 'Cain' and the boys very nicely.

7 EVOLUTION & THE CHICKEN & THE EGG

So what did come first, the chicken or the egg? For some people this is an unsolvable problem. This is life's great paradox. It seems at first glance, to be a circular argument that nobody can win. Here's the good news. I've got the answer.

An egg is simply a means of reproducing the creature that laid it, which for the sake of this debate, is a chicken. Having been laid, said egg undergoes a metamorphosis until it hatches out into a cute bundle of yellow chick which goes on to become an almost exact replica of its parents. OK so far? Of course it is; there's nothing contentious about all that is there?

Now let's look at the chicken. An adult chicken has, like every other creature on the planet, an in built desire to reproduce. This instinct (in almost every animal) is second only to the instinct for self-preservation. To fulfil this desire, a chicken lays an egg. However, if we remove the chicken's *desire* or *ability* to reproduce itself, we have removed the need for the egg. As a concept it becomes redundant which the chicken cannot. Therefore the chicken is the primary being, the egg secondary.

This is the conclusion reached by logical thinking applied to the chicken. In actual fact, science tells us that it is the other way around and that as all life evolved from a single celled creature, the egg came first.

The moral of this story is that however logical and substantial your argument is, science can, and often does, prove you wrong.

African Eve

Genetic scientists tells us that every Modern Human is related to a single female that ventured out of Africa with her family or tribe, some eighty thousand years ago. This conclusion was reached by studying mitochondrial DNA, (mDNA) a type of DNA that is passed on from mothers only through their female offspring and as a consequence, with DNA sequencing it is possible to turn back the clock as it were, to discover who was our nearest common female ancestor (ancestor to everyone on the planet.) Having done this, 'Mitochondrial Eve' was discovered. She is a distant relative of all of us.

This erstwhile lady lived in Africa 120,000 and 80,000 years ago, and is often referred to as 'African Eve'. (I wonder what her reaction to this statement would be!) Her offspring later migrated to what is now the Arabian Peninsula, along with other members of her tribe or family, and her children and their descendants went on to populate the entire world outside of Africa, replacing or absorbing all the other sub species who had gone before.

This African Eve is a very obvious candidate for Biblical Eve. The chart on page 67 depicts the genetic origins of our species, and their links to African Eve. Please note the location. I think this may be a good time to promote my

'Okavango' theory again.

Much DNA testing has taken place around the world, (see: The National Geographic Web site) and the conclusions that have been reached are fascinating. Apparently the gene pool of sub-Saharan Africa is much more diverse than that of anywhere else. This indicates that it has been functioning (people breeding) much longer than anywhere else, which is pretty conclusive evidence that the origins of the Human Race were located there. It also means, incidentally, that Mitochondrial Eve was a black African, and so, by extension, we are all from a black skinned family. Black lives really did matter back then; they were essential.

The older, more genetically diverse African population, is much nearer to our H.sapien ancestors than we are, (in genetic terms) who are all descended from African Eve and the original small group who exited Africa and populated the rest of the world. The antiquity of their DNA means that when the other sub species of humans disappeared, the gap was filled by the 'stay at home' H.sapien tribes.

Consider this….

We had fire. We cooked our meat, making it easier to digest and turn it into brain building stuff. It also enabled us to take time off from the chore of constantly looking for food and eating it. That spare time was not only used to make clothes and tools, but gave us time to dream, to build hopes for the future. The clothes we made kept us warm, enabling us to operate for longer in cold periods, increasing our efficiency in cool periods, and easily dispensed with when it was hot. No longer were we bound to the natural cycle. No longer servants to nature, with its 'red in tooth and claw' philosophy.

So here we are, wandering about the planet doing all the usual Homo sapien stuff, when all of a sudden, there's a huge bang. The biggest, loudest, most cataclysmic event our species has ever experienced. Toba, a super volcano in Indonesia erupted. About seventy two thousand years ago, this volcano erupted so violently and on such a scale that it is estimated that 90 per cent of life on earth was eradicated by the consequences of its eruption, including 90% of us. It's thought that as few as ten thousand individual H.s.sapiens and as few as 1,000 breeding pairs, survived the event and its aftermath. There was at the time an estimated total population of about one and a half million of us.

The event triggered a 6 to 10 year volcanic winter and possibly a 1,000-year cooling period immediately afterwards. Far away in the West, Cool Dude[16] cold climate specialist Neanderthal Man just soldiered on through what must have been to him, an inexplicably long and cold winter. Most of the world was plunged into an ice age. Vegetation buried beneath metres of volcanic ash and acid rain on a global scale. Yet we survived. It must have been truly horrific. Especially for those many thousands of miles away from the volcano that had no idea what had happened or why their world had been plunged literally overnight, into darkness, cold, and dust. I really feel for them. I am also filled with awe and admiration at their ability to survive. To keep on staying alive and making more humans was an incredible feat of endurance to which we all owe our existence.

We must also note that we were not the only ones to come through this holocaust. At least two other Hominin species survived it as well as us. So it wasn't Toba that gave us the planet. We must look elsewhere.

It was in these times that the ability of our species to manipulate its own environment was honed and polished to such an extent that we were able to dominate the planet. We took the tools and experience that we had, and we put it to use; desperate use. Succeed or die. It's in times such as these that most advances are made. Wars always bring new technology into the world. So do doomsday scenarios. So what happened to H.neanderthalensis, H.floresiensis, and H.erectus, the other Toba survivors?

Homo floresiensis lived through the Toba event and probably died out through loss of habitat and resources 50-60,000 years later. The much larger H.s.sapiens newcomers easily out did him in the quest for food and resources, and no doubt, he tasted nice too.

H.neanderthalensis in the west and the pocket of surviving H.erectus on Java may have suffered a different fate however, a fate that may well await us.

Extinction is a natural process, it is continuous and ruthless. Millions of species have died out during the history of Planet Earth. Some due to natural disaster and environmental change they couldn't adapt to, some due to epidemics of fatal diseases and others hunted to extinction. Most extinction occurs naturally. Prior to H.s.sapiens walking the Earth it's estimated that over 90% of all the species that have ever existed had become extinct.

World Domination

As the threat from the volcano ravaged world receded, times became easier and we flourished. Before long, farming, trade and industry were booming. Technology was invented as both a word and an industry, and the meat cooking, clothes wearing Homo s.sapien lived up to his name and did something incredible.

We have been in existence for about 2-300,000 years, maybe even slightly less, but our achievements in many disciplines far surpass those of our ancestors. We learned to fly, and not by evolutionary means taking millions of years, but by artificial means, by using tools, if you like.

Then, if that wasn't enough, we did something absolutely stupendous. Something so far from the ability of any other creature that has ever lived on earth, that it defies logic and belief. We left the planet and we went to the Moon, and only 70 years after first learning how to fly. To you and I that would be an exciting event (it was!), but it would not be surprising. After all, there are always rockets going off into space from somewhere. It happens almost weekly, but looking at it from the perspective of, say, a chimpanzee or a rabbit, we would seem like gods.

Crocs & Cookers

It's at this point that the situation of the Nile crocodile springs to my mind. That may sound a little odd to you perhaps, but you should have gathered by now that I have an odd sort of mind. It compares things and if it sees a similarity it homes in on it; likewise with contradictions or oddities such as the Nile Croc. Crocodylus Niloticus has been around for about 100 million years, give or take a month or two. H.habilis had to contend with them, for his fossilised bones have been found with croc bite marks in them, so he was being attacked and, presumably, eaten by them. Which begs the question (in my mind at least) if H.habilis evolved into H.erectus and thence into H.heidelbergensis during that period of time, then why has the fearsome Nile Croc remained unchanged? If time is the agent of evolution, then why is it that creatures such as the Nile Crocodile, the Great White Shark and even the humble Hedgehog, all remained unchanged, in some cases, for hundreds of millions of years? Surely they would have developed into different forms? There are many such examples of creatures and plants that have been quite happy to remain in their original form for millions of years. So why aren't the others?

Some argue that creatures only change when their environment changes or the circumstances surrounding their everyday lives alter. Again, this cannot be a consistent scenario, as the aforementioned creatures have witnessed everything from ice ages to the extinction of the dinosaurs when the Earth was hit by a six mile wide asteroid (The KT Event), not to mention the Toba eruption; hardly a stable foundation for them to build a future on. This theory of evolution seems to be a tad inconsistent to me.

Evolution is simply a series of random genetic accidents that sometimes give advantage to an individual and enables his or her offspring to better compete with or survive in their environment, than their contemporaries.

For example, the population which is at risk of the severe debilitating disease 'kuru' (the so called 'laughing disease' of Papua New Guinea) has an immune variant of the prion protein gene G127V. The frequency of this genetic variant is due to the survival of immune persons. Other reported evolutionary trends In other populations include a lengthening of the reproductive period, reduction in cholesterol levels, blood glucose and blood pressure, and a rising immunity to HIV. Let's hope it goes that way with Covid-19.

Your wisdom teeth are also a sign of evolution in us H. s.sapiens. Originally they were used to grind the fibrous roots and other tough items our ancestors collected for food, but with the advent of cooking, making food easier to chew, they have become redundant (and a problem) as our jaws receded and our faces became more gracile.

There is evidence that you and I are substantially different to our ancestors of 15,000 years ago. We have even evolved a second stomach. We call it 'the cooker'. Maybe you know it? It's that kitchen appliance Mum, or The Wife operates immediately prior to producing dinner. Our bodies have become so dependent upon cooked food, that if we were given a diet of raw food for any substantial period of time, we would practically starve to death. Try it. Just eat raw fruit and vegetables and unprocessed food for a few days. No hot drinks, just plain water. See how you feel. Not good I can assure you. This is direct evidence that our association with fire and cooked food has affected our development as a species, whereas our earliest ancestors thrived on such a diet.

Evolution is certainly not the 'Survival of the Fittest' system that it implies and is sometimes dubbed. Not by any means. H.heidelbergensis is, or was, proof of that.

One great debate used to be whether or not we are related to other primates (chimpanzees, gorillas etc.) through the Hominins that preceded us. Whilst we obviously have inherited some DNA from other sub species of Hominin (as much as 4% from Neanderthals) there is no solid proof that one sub species is directly related to another. Genetic studies have recently shown that Chimpanzees, whilst our closest *living* relative, (we share 98% of our DNA with them) are not direct ancestors but developed from a different branch of our common 'family tree'.

The fact remains that interbreeding amongst the closely related species (Erectus, Heidelbergensis, Neanderthalensis and us) was probably common place and this will skew any DNA research as individuals of one species may be related to individuals of another species, but the whole sub species may not be.

The answer to the question of whether or not we are related to monkeys, H.erectus, or any other primates, is one which will have to wait until DNA is extracted from an ancient fossil, or the Day of Judgement arrives. Either one will give us a definitive answer.

What is certain though is that H.s.sapiens succeeded in attaining the position of dominant life form after all the others of our species had faded into fossilised history. Even though H.erectus, H.neanderthalensis and others had left Africa before us, some of them better equipped than us, it was we alone who survived and prevailed.

We were favoured by some circumstance that bypassed our peers and gave us free reign and sovereignty. The Million Dollar question is, of course, what was it? It wasn't our superior strength or agility. We were second rate in these departments. Nor was it even our big brain. Others had the capacity too.

Our very weakness and slower speed threatened to push us into oblivion. 'Evolution' had dealt us a losing hand compared to our contemporaries. We were coming in last and it was time to beat the system.

This is the point at which I throw away my copy of Darwin's much acclaimed publication, 'The Origin of Species by Natural Selection' and the theory of Survival of the Fittest. Whilst Darwin's publication and the theory contained therein were perfectly acceptable when it was first launched upon the world, it would seem now that this theory is not the constant that everyone considers it to be.

We are living proof that it is a faulty and for us, an easily bypassed system. Darwin was wrong. It is our very survival that proves this. We beat the system with our devious brain and our cunning. We are the result of a *failure* of the natural system; an aberration in an otherwise natural world. Instead of the biggest, strongest, best suited Hominin (H.heidelbergensis?) coming to power, his weaker, but more treacherous sibling used artificial means to beat the competition and usurped the throne. From that day about 120,000 years ago, to this, we have cheated nature. Disagree? Think about the current Coronavirus pandemic. Consider our position without man made vaccines. We'd be very vulnerable as a species.

You can't go to The Moon without a fur coat

Something's amiss. I get the distinct impression that we don't fit in here. Unlike the rest of the citizens of this beautiful blue planet, we have not 'evolved' in sync with nature. The laws of natural selection do not (fully) apply to us. We're different. And not by evolution, for without making ourselves a 'fur coat', we couldn't have even invented the wheel, never mind gone to the moon. Without making ourselves clothes to keep us warm, we'd still be confined to the African Savannah. Instead we exploited the comparative 'honesty' of the planet and its inhabitants for our own advantage with no regard to the consequences. We have usurped the throne, and have enslaved the planet and its inhabitants.

Let me explain what I mean by the 'honesty' of the natural system. There are no other creatures that are not perfectly well equipped to deal with the circumstances in which they live. I ask you, is there one, just one inhabitant of this planet of ours which cannot survive here without the need to resort to artificial means of life support? If they are cold they have fur, if they are wet they have gills. If they need shelter they have a shell, dig a hole, or steal someone else's. That describes the natural order of things. But here *we* are.

Strip us of the artefacts we make ourselves, by means of our own technology, and we die in a matter of days. 'Natural Selection' weeds us out of The Garden in no time at all. Don't tell me about cave dwelling either. Those other Hominins that made a habit of cave dwelling are gone. Toes turned up and just pictures in a text book. We soon gave it up as a bad job, moving on to huts and then houses. Besides, you won't find enough holes in the ground for seven billion of us, or even enough forage to feed us.

We stand alone as the undisputed rulers of this planet. Not even the dinosaurs, who ruled the place for hundreds of millions of years, got anywhere near our mastery of the world. They never even managed to build a skateboard, let alone go to the moon. But they never cheated the system and changed the environment in which they lived to suit themselves. It's only H.s.sapiens who makes up the rules as he goes along. Everything else stays within the natural order of things even when it means they die.

When you hear anthropologists and others talking about

the 'success' of the Human race, you are listening to the inflated ego of a species bragging about its sovereignty over its environment and other species. This is the dictator telling the populace how wonderful the regime is.

It's been argued that human evolution has accelerated since, and as a result of, the development of agriculture some 10,000 years ago. It's claimed that this has resulted in substantial genetic differences between different current human populations. However, because of the genetic Russian roulette that is enacted every time a new individual is conceived when egg and sperm meet; and because of the DNA recombination that ensues, it is possible that 'evolution' can work in the opposite direction.

I believe it (see: Adam's Curse by Prof. Brian Sykes) is responsible for the demise of some of the early Hominins, and will eventually account for H.s.sapiens too, if climate change doesn't do for us first. There is awaiting us, a pitfall we cannot as yet avoid, a scenario that looks as though it could put an end to the 7 million year old Hominin family once and for all.

We may avoid extinction by means of applying our technology (cheating the system again) but this, alas, was not an option for other the members of the Hominin family whom I believe suffered this fate and they have paid the price.

They're just fossils on a museum shelf.

8 MODERN HUMANS: WHAT WE ARE

Kingdom:	Animal
Phylum:	Chordate
Class:	Mammal
Order:	Primate
Family:	Hominin
Genus:	Homo
Species:	H.sapien
Sub species:	H.s.sapien

Humans. People. You, me and the guy next door. Yes, you, the higher mammalian life form with the opposable thumbs....

Some 200 to 300,000 years ago, on the savannahs of East Africa, there emerged from the mist and populace of preceding time, a creature that was to change the face of the planet and affect the lives of every living thing on it. This newcomer was a primate of the genus Homo. Homo sapien to give him his full title. That's right, us.

The name Homo as a genus of the order Primates was first recorded as long ago as 1797, but the name 'Homo sapien' was first used in 1802, in William Turton's translation of Linnæus, coined in modern Latin from homo "man" (technically "male human,") but in logical and scholastic writing "human being;" and sapien, "be wise".

To distinguish us from the earlier archaic Homo sapiens (version 1.0) to our Modern Homo sapiens (version 1.1) the title became Homo sapiens sapiens, the human being who was the wisest of the wise. Bit of a paradoxical title if you ask me.

It's interesting to note that according to legend, Adam and Eve were expelled from the Garden of Eden for eating the fruit from the tree of knowledge. Consuming this fruit gave them the knowledge of good and evil. This would make them 'wise' would it not? They would then be humans who were knowledgeable, or 'wise', i.e. Homo sapiens.

No one except myself and Vanessa Hayes will say exactly where H.s.sapiens came from, and not even we can say exactly when he appeared, but it's a fair guess that he was the product of a combination of interbreeding between other forms of Hominin, and genetic mutation coming of age in the wetlands of what is now Botswana. By 180,000 years ago, he was firmly established as a resident of the Dark Continent. Unfortunately for Archbishop Usher, we can now prove that his timescale was somewhat flawed.

Paleoanthropologists have reliable proof in the form of fossils that the first Modern Humans (Homo sapiens sapien) were roaming around the East African landscape some 120,000 years ago, and that the earliest forms of Hominins predated them by some 6 million years. For thousands of years Homo s.sapiens made a living on the plains of East

Africa, during which time he developed his tool making skills and mastered not only the grassland environment of the savannah, but also the coastal plains of the Indian and probably the Atlantic Oceans. By 120,000 years ago he was an accomplished fire using, clothes wearing, tool making hunter-gatherer who in all

Migration Routes Out of Africa
1. Homo s.sapien. 2. Neanderthals. 3. Homo erectus
(Numbers indicate how many years ago)

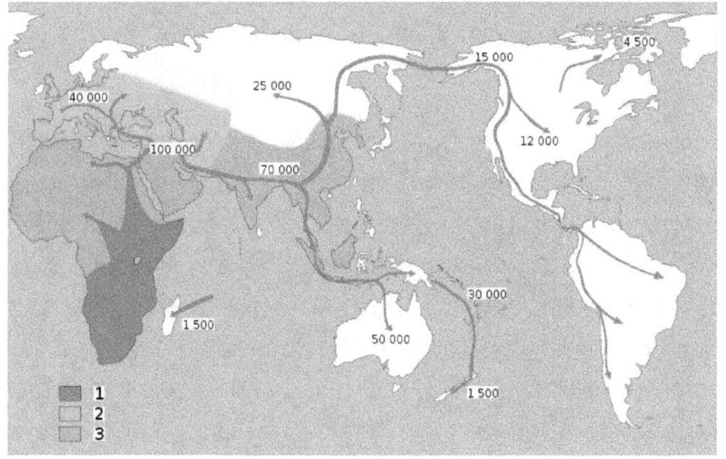

probability used primitive boats of various design. Now we come to the interesting bit.

About 80,000 years ago H.s.sapiens started his second major 'Out of Africa' migration and ventured into the larger world beyond. They found their way across the Arabian Peninsula and from here they branched out in several directions. They went east into the Sub-Continent, Indonesia and China, then West into Europe, and North to the Russian Steppes.   Eventually H.s.sapiens made it to Australia, The Americas, Polynesia and then only 1500 years ago to New Zealand.

He was not alone though. Many hundreds of thousands of years before, possibly as long ago as 1.5 million years ago, another Hominin, H.erectus, had migrated from Africa and had colonised many areas of the world. H.heidelbergensis also migrated out of Africa, and he too had spread over most of Europe and much of Asia. His fossilised bones have been found in England and have been dated as 740,000 years old.

There was H.neanderthalensis in Western Europe and the Middle East, and also the little man of Indonesia, H.floresiensis, but it took H.s.sapiens to conquer the ocean waves and settle the Pacific region. There is evidence, such as the early settlement of Australia between 40 and 60,000 years ago, and the discovery of stone hand axes in Crete dated from between 700,000 and 130,000 years ago, that suggests that boats have been used since very ancient times, although whether it was H.heidelbergensis or H.erectus who first used them is uncertain.

The dating of the tools in Crete of 130,000 years ago would suggest it wasn't H.s.sapiens, as he would not have started his migration by then. Crete has been isolated from any other mainland (by 40 miles of sea) for about 5 million years, so who ever used the tools had to come by boat or he was quite a swimmer!

H.s.sapiens colonizing adventure ebbed and flowed, but after about 80,000 years ago, he was a major figure on the world stage. H.heidelbergensis had vanished sometime after H.sapiens had first emerged, H.erectus was dwindling into oblivion and the Hobbit was confined to a small island in Indonesia.

H.s.sapiens survived, spreading across from the sub-continent to central Europe and the west, eventually replacing Neanderthal man, who it seems, made his last stand in a cave on the rock of Gibraltar.

Ten thousand years ago everything changed again. The Agricultural Revolution sounded the death knell for the hunter gatherer, and Mankind set off on an irreversible downhill slide towards his doom. Never again could we live the life that nature intended. We were shackled by population growth to fulfill the other part of Adam's Curse, to till the soil in a never ending battle to feed a constantly growing population. This became a vicious circle that even today we are unable to break.

It's all in the Genes

Look around at the population of the supermarket next time you go shopping. Of course there will be white skinned people and brown skinned people and some very dark or black skinned people. There are tall people and short people. There are hairy people and, well, not so hairy people.

There are also people that are what we call 'thick set' with heavier facial features than we consider usual. All of these people have inherited the way they look from their parents. Apart from the normal variations in the population (wherever it may be) some people may have also inherited recessive genes that have been dormant for many generations and have only just found a mate to bring them to light. The taller amongst us may well be showing an echo of our relationship to H.heidelbergensis, and his two and a half metre stature.

Thick set features may well be a distant reminder of our ancestor's relationship with H.neanderthalensis and his heavier build. But where did the lightly built individuals get their genes from?

Homo floresiensis is an obvious contender, but standing at about a metre high, it is very unlikely that they successfully mated with any other Homo species, being as they were, something like half the size of the others. The result of any up close and personal encounter probably ended up as them being a meal rather than a mate.   Interbreeding was not impossible of course.

There have been many small girls who have given birth to a baby conceived with much larger men, but without the assistance of modern medical science, very few mothers of their size, or their offspring, would have survived in the distant past. There certainly wouldn't have been enough of them to account for the many millions of H.s.sapien who fall into the 'lightly built' category. Their existence must be the result of something else.

Environmental selection has been at work. Not enough of the right food generation to generation to promote long bones; climate conditions favouring smaller bodies and social or sexual preferences dictating population traits. The way we are has been moulded by many factors over many generations and will continue to be so for a long time to come.

Adam's Curse

I've borrowed this heading from a book by a hero of mine, the late Dr. Bryan Sykes, which I can thoroughly recommend. He was a Professor of Human Genetics at Oxford University and had a leading role in researching Human origins over the years. According to his research, the future of Homo s.sapien is in doubt. In his book, 'Adam's Curse', he expounds the theory that the human 'Y' chromosome is being driven into extinction by the very process of reproduction. He tells us that every time a 'Y' chromosome is passed on from father to son, it suffers a little damage, and it has, over the generations, become smaller and smaller, effecting the fertility of male humans the world over.

Male fertility is decreasing markedly and it may not just be a result of modern lifestyles. Bryan Sykes tells us that because of the damage inflicted upon the 'Y' chromosomes during the recombination of DNA when a baby is conceived; it is becoming less likely that males will be born. This will eventually lead to the disappearance of the chromosome altogether, leaving us in a world with no men. Remember the default situation? No 'Y' and it's a female. Well it seems that this situation is becoming more and more frequent and in about 5000 generations, only female children will be born. If we take an average of 20 years per generation, then it's game over in 100,000 years. That will have given us 350,000 years, somewhat less than the average (478,000 years) for a Hominin species

The poor old 'Y' chromosome is being battered to death. The advent of In-Vitro Fertilization (IVF) and the Assisted Reproductive Technologies (ARTs) has helped thousands of otherwise infertile couples to have children over the last few decades. Even so, 10% of couples are left with an inability to have children because IVF does not work for everyone. The number of couples seeking medical attention for infertility related problems has rapidly grown in recent years. In fact, male fertility has decreased by a worrying 40% over the last century.

 From the Islamic Tradition

(Bukhari) Anas ibn Malik told this Hadith (reported by Ibn Majh and Bukhari) spoken by the Prophet:

"I shall tell you a Hadith which I heard from the Messenger of Allah, and which no one will tell you after me. I heard him say,

'Amongst the signs of the Hour will be the disappearance of knowledge and the appearance of ignorance. Adultery will be prevalent and the drinking of wine will be common. The number of men will decrease and the number of women will

increase until there will be fifty women to be looked after by one man.'

Education, especially about religion which is the topic in this passage, is becoming more widespread, but the overall quality of it is dropping. Just look on You Tube or consider the number of Bible 'versions'. You can buy a bottle of wine in a super market for a few pounds or dollars or whatever. It's cheap and commonplace. Adultery and sexual promiscuity are far more prevalent than they were even a hundred years ago, and now we have the good Doctor's revelation of Adam's Curse. Who would have thought it would all be so obvious to a seventh century prophet?

This self-destruction is brought about by the way we breed, which also happened to be the same way of course, that all the other, extinct members of our family used to reproduce. Why is it, I wonder, that it is presented as a mystery as to why all the others disappeared from the face of the Earth? If it can happen to us, why shouldn't it have happened to them too? It all seems perfectly logical to me.

Let's hark back to the Bible for a moment, shall we? Adam and Eve are living in the Garden of Eden. All is Hunky Dory until Eve is persuaded by The Serpent to eat the fruit of the Tree of Knowledge. She shares it with Adam and, inevitably, God finds out and his judgement on the couple for disobeying his commands is pretty harsh. In short they are chucked out of Paradise, condemned to death, (as opposed to living forever in the Garden) and in the meantime, set one against the other in the eternal 'Battle of the Sexes'.

Here it is that we find the original 'Adam's Curse'.

Holy Bible (King James Version) Genesis 3:2 – 3

3:2 And the woman said unto the serpent, We may eat of the fruit of the trees of the garden

3:3 But of the fruit of the tree which is in the midst of the garden, God hath said, Ye shall not eat of it, neither shall ye touch it, lest ye die.

But of course, as we all know, Adam and Eve ignored God. The pertinent part of their punishment is documented as follows:

Holy Bible (King James Version) Genesis 3:15-16

3:15 And I will put enmity between thee and the woman, and between thy seed and her seed; it shall bruise thy head, and thou shalt bruise his heel.

3:16 Unto the woman he said, I will greatly multiply thy sorrow and thy conception; in sorrow thou shalt bring forth children; and thy desire shall be to thy husband, and he shall rule over thee.

Holy Bible (King James Version) Genesis 3:19

3:19 In the sweat of thy face shalt thou eat bread, till thou return unto the ground; for out of it wast thou taken: for dust thou art, and unto dust shalt thou return.

It takes very little imagination to see that the references to 'seed' concern the 'Y' chromosome bearing sperm, and the 'X' chromosome bearing egg. There certainly seems to be enmity between the two, and the 'Y' chromosome is losing. Looking at verse 3 we see the death threat, and in 19, we see that Adam, or if you will, Mankind, is destined to return to dust, to disappear. Here again the Scriptures (chillingly) parallel science.

The reference to dying doesn't necessarily refer to Adam and Eve as individuals, as you may think. Genesis has already shown us that Adam and Eve were expelled from the Garden of Eden before they found 'The Tree of Life' which would have given them immortality. No, this reference tells us that ALL men are doomed to die. Dr. Sykes and Genesis agree on that one then. But what of the other Hominin sub species? What of the other Hominins that roamed Africa, Asia and Europe.

Sometimes they walked along side us; some of them pre dated us by millions of years. History tells us their story. They're gone. Of course poor old H.erectus, H.heidelbergensis and H.neanderthalensis didn't have recourse to the marvels of the genetics laboratory or IVF treatment like Modern Man, and, presumably succumbed to the onslaught of continual DNA recombination during reproduction. Admittedly some of them lasted a long time and they also wore clothes, used fire and tools, but they just didn't hack it did they? They were lacking a certain something. Maybe they weren't such good tailors or Astronauts as we are.

Eve's two daughters and the Genetic Haplogroups.

Dear old Great Grandma Eve, (whoever she was), must have been blessed with at least two healthy daughters. This is evident by the number of genetic 'tribes' (Haplogroups), our gene pool consists of. On page 67 you will see just a few examples; L, L1 L2, L3, M and N. I am a member of haplogroup J. If Eve had given birth to just one daughter then there would only be one Haplogroup, L0. The fact that we have many proves that her genes were divided between at least two female offspring which then kept on dividing to give us our current genetically diverse gene pool.

If you are considering having your DNA sequenced by one of these specialist companies that have sprung up in recent years, bear in mind that unless they tell you which haplogroup you are a member of, you're wasting your money. Finding out where your great grand parents came from is not the purpose of DNA sequencing. Finding out how old your direct relatives have lived on the planet and where they originated thousands of years ago is what it's all about. Far more interesting too.

The Parable of the Ford Escort

Once upon a time there were two people who had just retired from work. They took some of their life's savings and went to the big Ford dealer in their town. Having looked at all the cars, they decide to buy a silver grey Ford Escort.

'It's not too big, but it's comfortable and cheap enough for a couple of pensioners to run....' said the husband to the salesman. '....and it will probably do us for the rest of our days.'

For several years the car was driven carefully and responsibly, never mistreated and always serviced on time. They used it mainly for visiting their children and going shopping. It made their lives so much easier than having to get the bus everywhere. Then one day the old man died, and his wife, who couldn't drive, advertised the car for sale in the local paper. A young couple, who had just had a baby and couldn't afford a new car, decided it was perfect for them.

'It's always been looked after properly. My husband was very careful with it, and it's always been kept in the garage.' the old lady told the couple.

Off went the young couple in their new car. They put a baby seat in the back for the little one, and it served them very well. Then one day the wife had another baby, and so another baby seat was installed. If there wasn't a bag in the boot with nappies and baby things, there were bags of shopping. It was a busy life for the little family car. When the third baby was on the way, the Ford Escort just wasn't big enough anymore, so they sold it and bought a bigger car.

The new owner was the trainee mechanic from the garage where the couple took the car to be serviced. By now the car was ten years old, and looking a little tired. However, it was just what the young mechanic wanted. He re-sprayed the car with a metallic silver paint, fitted it with low profile tyres, renovated the engine and fitted a turbo charger and turned the little car into something of a hot rod! He took it to car rallies and hot rod shows. Inevitably, before too long, the passenger seat was regularly occupied by his new girlfriend. And the young mechanic was so very grateful to Henry Ford for making it all possible for him.

The moral of this story is that no matter what use the car is put to, it's still only a car. It may have started out as a fairly sedentary machine, but eventually the time came when it had to move on. It evolved into a family car, busy and part of a growing family. Eventually though, the family out grew it and it had to evolve again. This time, it moved into a completely different scenario, far more technically advanced than when it started out in its career, even though it was now quite an old car.

The same is true of our Human body. For thousands of millennia it has been evolving and like the car, has passed through many stages. It has been put to different uses by different owners, but it's still just a body. What matters is the use it's put to. So what if it was once a hairy cave dwelling primitive man? Nowadays it's something of a hot rod, and we are the young owner. H.erectus and the others have passed this body on to us and we've taken it and turned it into bit of a racer.

We just have to be careful where and how we drive it....

9 HALL OF FAME

We cannot really discuss the history of Mankind without including those species that, at some dim and distant point in history may have been included in our body's lineage. I think they deserve a mention too, don't you? The inclusion of this chapter is basically for your information. If you have got this far, then you obviously have an interest in our history. The ones most pertinent to this book I have described in detail, but others appear only in the listings below. It must be remembered that some of these individuals lived a very long time ago, and I mean a *very* long time ago. Below is an indicator of who comes where in history. It is not meant to be a 'family tree' or an indication that any one species is related to, or has evolved from another, nor even a complete nor accurate picture of the time the species lived.

Homo floresiensis	95,000 to 3,000? y.a
Homo s.sapien	200-300,000 y.a to present
Homo naledi	235,000 to 335,000 y.a
Homo denisova	? to 30,000 y.a ?
Homo neanderthalensis	400,000 to 24,000 y.a
Homo luzonensis	700,000 to ? ya.
Homo heidelbergensis	800,000 to 200,000 y.a
Homo antecessor	1,200,000 to 500,000 y.a
Homo ergaster	1,800.000 to 500,000 y.a
Homo erectus	2,000,000 to 70,000 y.a
Homo habilis	2,800,000 to 1,400,000 y.a
Australopithecus afarensis	3,200,000 to ? y.a (Lucy)
Australopithecus africanus	3,300,000 to 3,100,000
Sahelanthrop tchadensis	7,000,000-6,000,000 y.a

If I omitted to mention you and yours, please accept my apologies. There are other fossils that may represent other species, however there is so much uncertainty and debate about them I have not included them in this list. Here's a run-down of our main Hominin family members. Eyes down and look in for a quick family history lesson.

All the species mentioned above are represented by a relatively small number of fossils. In fact there are only two species that are represented by what is anything like a complete skeleton. They are the famous 'Lucy' (Australopithecus afarensis) and 'Turkana Boy' (Homo ergaster). 'Lucy' is not part of our alleged ancestry, being an Australopithecus, and 'Turkana Boy' lived some 1.8 million years ago.

Many of the other fossil specimens are just a skull and a few bones. For example the complete collection of fossils for Orrorin tugenensis comprises: "the posterior part of mandible in two pieces; a symphysis and several isolated teeth; three fragments of femurs; a partial humerus; a proximal phalanx; and a distal thumb phalanx". A very small percentage of the complete skeleton.

Don't labour under the misconception that there are plenty of samples for the scientists to study and pronounce on. These ancient fossilised bones are extremely rare, often small in size and very valuable.

Homo erectus

Homo erectus (from the Latin 'erigere', to set upright) is an extinct species of Hominin that originated in Africa and spread as far as India, China and Java from the end of the Pliocene epoch to the later Pleistocene, about 1.8 to 1.3 million years ago.

The first theory is that Homo erectus migrated from Africa during the Early Pleistocene, possibly as a result of the operation of the Saharan pump (see Glossary of Terms), around 2.0 million years ago, and dispersed throughout much of the Old World. Fossilized remains 1.8 to 1 million years old have been found in Africa (e.g., Lake Turkana and Olduvai Gorge), Europe (Georgia, Spain), Indonesia (e.g., Sangiran and Trinil), Vietnam, China (e.g., Shaanxi) and India.

Throughout much of the 20th century, anthropologists debated the role of H.erectus in human evolution. Early in the century, however, due to discoveries on Java and at Zhoukoudian, it was believed that modern humans first evolved in Asia. A few naturalists (Charles Darwin most prominent amongst them) predicted that humans' earliest ancestors were African: he pointed out that chimpanzees and gorillas, who are human relatives, live only in Africa. From 1950s to 1970s, however, numerous fossils from East Africa yielded evidence that the oldest Hominins originated there.

It is now believed that Homo erectus is a descendant of

earlier genera such as Ardipithecus and Australopithecus, or early Homo species such as Homo habilis or Homo ergaster.

The sexual dimorphism between males and females was slightly greater than seen in Homo s.sapien, with males being about 25% larger than females. However, their dimorphism is drastically less than that of the earlier Australopithecus genus. There is no fossil evidence of any clothing that that Homo erectus might have worn. Homo erectus was a reasonably sophisticated tool user, and there is evidence of both complex social units and limited mastery of fire, so it is conceivable that Homo erectus used animal hides and possibly even stitched them into forms of clothing. It is unlikely that they produced anything woven or textile-like, though they may have bound grasses or reeds together for various purposes. In terms of survival, Homo erectus was the most successful of the Hominin species at nearly 2 million years. He colonised Africa, Europe and Asia making the use of clothing and fire essential.

Homo heidelbergensis (The Giants in the Land)

Homo heidelbergensis ("Heidelberg Man") named after the University of Heidelberg is an extinct species of the genus Homo which may be the direct ancestor of both Homo neanderthalensis in Europe and Homo s.sapien. The best evidence found for these Hominins date between 600,000 and 400,000 years ago. Homo heidelbergensis stone tool technology was very close to that of tools used by Homo erectus.

Homo heidelbergensis are likely to be descended from the morphologically very similar Homo ergaster from Africa, but because Homo heidelbergensis had a larger brain-case — with a <u>typical cranial volume of 1100–1400 cm³ overlapping the 1350 cm³ average of modern humans </u> — and had more advanced tools and behaviour, it has been given a separate species classification. <u>The species was tall, 1.8 m (6 ft.) **on average**, and **more muscular than modern humans**</u>. According to Professor Lee R. Berger of the University of Witwatersrand, numerous fossil bones indicate **<u>some populations of Heidelbergensis were "giants"</u>** <u>routinely over 2.13 m (7 ft.) tall</u> and inhabited South Africa between 0.5 million and 300,000 years ago. In 2005 flint tools and teeth from the water vole Mimomys Savini, a key dating species, were found in the cliffs at Pakefield near Lowestoft in Suffolk. This suggests that Hominins can be dated in England to 700,000 years ago, potentially a cross between Homo Antecessor and Homo Heidelbergensis.

<u>Homo neanderthalensis</u>

'Neanderthal Man' is an extinct member of the Homo genus known from Pleistocene specimens found in Europe and parts of western and central Asia. Neanderthals are classified either as a subspecies (or race) of modern humans (Homo s.sapien neanderthalensis) or as a separate human species (Homo neanderthalensis). The first proto-Neanderthal traits appeared in Europe as early as 400,000-350,000 years ago. Proto-Neanderthal traits are occasionally grouped with another phenetic 'species', Homo heidelbergensis, or a migrant form, Homo rhodesiensis.

Neanderthals disappeared in Asia by 50,000 years ago and in Europe by about 28,000 years ago, with no further individuals having enough Neanderthal morphological traits to be considered as part of Homo neanderthalensis.

Genetic evidence suggests interbreeding took place with Homo s.sapien (anatomically modern humans) between roughly 80,000 and 50,000 years ago in the Middle East, resulting in 1-4% of the genome of people from Eurasia having been contributed by Neanderthals. Early Neanderthals lived in the last glacial age for a span of about 100,000 years. Because of the damage inflicted by the glaciers on the Neanderthal sites, not much is known about the early species. Countries where their remains are known include most of Europe south of the line of glaciation, (roughly along the 50th parallel north), most of Western Europe, including the south coast of Great Britain, Central Europe and the Balkans, some sites in the Ukraine and in western Russia. Outside of Europe their remains have been discovered in the Zagros Mountains of the Iran/Turkish border and in the Levant.

Neanderthal fossils have not been found to date in Africa, but there have been finds rather close to Africa, both at Gibraltar and in the Levant. At some Levantine sites, Neanderthal remains, in fact, are dated after the same sites were vacated by Homo s.sapien. Mammal fossils of the same time period show cold-adapted animals were present alongside these Neanderthals in this region of the Eastern Mediterranean. This implies Neanderthals were better adapted biologically to cold weather than Homo s.sapien and at times displaced H.s.sapien in parts of the Middle East when the climate got cold enough.

H.s.sapiens appear to have been the only human type in the Nile River Valley during these periods, and Neanderthals are not known to have ever lived south-west of modern Israel.

The youngest Neanderthal finds include Hyaena Den (UK), considered older than 30,000 years ago, while the Vindija (Croatia) Neanderthals have been re-dated to between 33,000 and 32,000 years ago. No definite specimens younger than 30,000 years ago have been found; however, evidence of fire by Neanderthals at Gibraltar indicate they may have survived there until 24,000 years ago. The Neanderthals disappear from the fossil record after about 25,000 years ago. The last traces of their culture have been found in Gorham's Cave on the remote south-facing coast of Gibraltar, dated 30,000 to 24,500 years ago. It was either through being unable to cope with climate change or competition from Homo s.sapien, possibly a combination of both factors that pushed them over the edge. I propose that genetic degeneration (Adam's Curse) would have been the main reason for their extinction.

Corinne Simoneti at Vanderbilt University, in Nashville and her team have researched medical records of 28,000 people of European descent and have come to the conclusion that the presence of Neanderthal DNA segments in their genome may be associated with the likelihood to suffer depression more frequently. Obviously being a Neanderthal wasn't much fun.

Homo floresiensis

Homo floresiensis ("Flores Man", nicknamed "hobbit") is a possible species, now extinct, in the genus Homo. The remains were discovered in 2004 on the island of Flores in Indonesia. Partial skeletons of nine individuals have been recovered, including one complete skull. These remains have been the subject of intense research to determine whether they represent a species distinct from modern humans, and the progress of this scientific controversy has been closely followed by the news media at large. This Hominin is remarkable for its small body and brain and for its survival until relatively recent times. Alongside the skeletal remains were stone tools from 94,000 to 13,000 years ago. Scientists have determined that the first skeleton they found belongs to a species of human completely new to science. Named Homo floresiensis, after the island on which it was found, the tiny human has also been dubbed by dig workers as the "hobbit," after the small men from the Lord of the Rings books.

The original skeleton, a female, stood at just 1 meter (3.3 feet) tall, weighed about 25 kilograms (55 pounds), and was around 30 years old at the time of her death 18,000 years ago. The skeleton was found in the same sediment deposits on Flores that have also been found to contain stone tools and the bones of dwarf elephants, giant rodents, and Komodo dragons, lizards that can grow to 10 feet (3 meters) and that still live today.

Homo floresiensis has been described as one of the most

spectacular discoveries in paleoanthropology in half a century, and the most extreme human ever discovered. The species inhabited Flores as recently as 13,000 years ago, which means it would have lived at the same time as modern humans.

"To find that as recently as perhaps 13,000 years ago, there was another upright, bipedal—although small-brained—creature walking the planet at the same time as modern humans is as exciting as it was unexpected," said Peter Brown, a paleoanthropologist at the University of New England in New South Wales, Australia.

"It is totally unexpected," said Chris Stringer, director of the Human Origins program at the Natural History Museum in London.

"To have early humans on the remote island of Flores is surprising enough. That some are only about a meter tall with a chimp-size brain is even more remarkable. That they were still there less than 20,000 years ago, and that modern humans must have met them, is astonishing."

The researchers estimate that the tiny people lived on Flores from about 95,000 years ago until at least 13,000 years ago. The scientists base their theory on charred bones and stone tools found on the island. The blades, perforators, points, and other cutting and chopping utensils were apparently used to hunt big (?) game. More recent finds indicate that Homo floresiensis may well have been around until as recently as 3,000 years ago.

Homo sapiens sapiens

Modern Humans. Us. Despite being physically inferior to their predecessors and many other species, H.s.sapiens are the planet's apex predators and dominant terrestrial life form.

In September 2019, scientists reported the computerised determination, based on 260 CT scans, of a virtual skull shape of the last common human ancestor to modern humans and suggested that modern humans arose between 260,000 and 350,000 years ago through a merging of populations in East and South Africa.

For an accurate physical description, look in a mirror. Homo sapiens sapiens are infamous for their desire to understand, influence and adapt their environment, seeking to explain and manipulate phenomena through science, philosophy and religion. This natural curiosity has led to the development of advanced tools and skills, which are passed down culturally. ***Humans are the only living species known*** to build fires, cook their food, clothe themselves, and use numerous technologies. We are the only species to have left the planet and the only species to purposely and knowingly endanger its own existence.

Food for Thought.....

Here are a few statistics from human history and a few from the present.

3,600,000	Age of earliest fossil human footprints
125,000	Generations since first Homo species
8,500	Generations of Homo s.sapien
110 Bn	Aprox no. of people who have lived
103 Bn	Aprox no. of those who are dead
44 Bn	Aprox no. who died before first birthday
7 Bn	Aprox no. still living
100,000	Aprox no. of years to our extinction
10 years	Average Homo s.sapien life expectancy
10,000	Number of human languages
100	Hours for pop. to grow by one million
12	Men to the Moon (384,400kms)
22	People to the deepest Ocean (Pacific Challenger Deep 10.91kms)
2	People to both Space and Challenger Deep (Kathy Sullivan 2020. Richard Garriott 2021)
11	**The Number of children under age five to die every minute from disease or starvation**

An Epitaph for a (different) Species.

A long time ago in a place far away, a solitary Neanderthal woman sat on a mountain top. A hundred metres below her, in a large cave, her baby and her mate lay dead. The sickness that took them had ravaged their starving little community but had spared her and she was the last surviving one.

She looked out across the landscape to her North, and then scanned the horizon towards the South and what we call the Mediterranean Sea. She raised her hand to shield her eyes from the afternoon Sun. She had to find another tribe. It was her only hope. But where were they?

Where was everyone else?

10 SUMMING UP HUMANITY

The Judeo Christian scriptures tell us God created the Earth, the Universe, and everything in it. Before this there was nothing. Some versions of Genesis even suggest that before the creation of the Universe, even God was intangible (the Word) and that it was only after the decision to create the Universe was taken that He became a substantial being (i.e. a being, but of unknown substance).

We are obliged by theologians to consider the idea that God is an unknown quantity, able to build, create, substantiate, without apparent means or materials, but when this concept is compared to the result of His work, the whole theory starts to take on a rather odd dimension, don't you think.

There is absolutely nothing in the natural world that is unexplainable, illogical, or mathematically impossible. Those questions which have puzzled mankind for centuries (e.g. Is the world flat? Does the Sun go around the Earth?) have eventually come to be resolved and have been found to have very logical and sophisticated mechanisms, and reasons for being. It would seem odd, would it not, that these fabulous and wonderfully sophisticated and integrated systems were the result of a mystical and unexplainable process, enacted by an equally mystical and unexplainable being?

If it were suggested, (it has, many times) that God were a mathematician, it would, in my opinion, be a perfectly reasonable assumption to make. The Laws of Physics dictate and explain the whole operation of our Universe, and the Earth's various ecosystems, without any support or assistance by mystical or unexplainable sources. So why is it assumed that the whole process was instigated by a mysterious and magical figure, in an equally mysterious and magical manner?

As an explanation several thousand years ago to illiterate and superstitious peoples without the benefit (?) of technology, the story of The Creation as it is written in the Scriptures would be a fairly good answer to questions about our origin, but today, appear to be rooted firmly in the realm of Fairy Stories. Their belief in Magic and the Supernatural would today be swept aside by a wave of scientific knowledge.

So do we write the account of Creation off as just that, a Fairy Story? Absolutely not. As we have seen in earlier chapters there are too many explanations about life and living that appear in various scriptures to discount them as uninformed.

All this discussion about Adam and Eve, and their sons and their wives is all very well, but it doesn't paint a very clear picture about where we all came from does it? Most paleoanthropologists agree that H.sapiens originated in Africa and started his successful migration into the rest of the world in two waves, the first 120,000 years ago and the second, more successful one, about 80,000 years ago. Ten thousand years later, the super volcano Toba erupted and wiped out all but a few of us, who then went on to re-populate the rest of the planet. That's all pretty clear and simple. No spouse paradoxes, no mythical creatures or supernatural happenings. Everything is writ large in the fossil and geological records; all in accordance with the Laws of Nature and Physics.

Let me ask the Believers amongst you; do you not consider that the Truth is God's way? That if it's Natural and of this Universe it's of God's will, is it not of His design and making? According to your religion and theory, nothing can exist unless it is so. Given that the fossil finds made by paleoanthropologists and the discoveries made by the Physicists and Cosmologists are (in most cases) true, how can they not be of God's will and making? Please don't start an argument at this point about Satanic or human conspiracies, or begin to expostulate on the inadequacies of, or the disagreements in, academic circles. You will succeed only in showing yourself as an unthinking follower of someone else's dogma.

The Scientists amongst you, how can you ignore the scriptures? Haven't you bothered to read them? Those notable scribes of old obviously had knowledge of events that had taken place long before they lived, and they also had an insight into some things that today's technology has only just managed to discover. I am not familiar with Jewish teachings, but have a little knowledge of the Christian Holy Bible, (or at least one of them) and the Muslim's Holy Qur'an (Koran).

Here, for example, is an account of conception in the Holy Qur'an,

Holy Qur'an, Chapter 22 (The Pilgrimage) Verse 5

22:5 We have created you from dust, then from a drop of seed, then from a clot, then from a little lump of flesh shapely and shapeless, that We may make (it) clear for you. And We cause what We will to remain in the wombs for an appointed time, and afterward We bring you forth as infants, then (give you growth) that ye attain your full strength.

It describes the process as being instigated by a 'drop of seed'. I am reliably informed that the Arabic used describes what we now know to be a single sperm, but I think the text above is quite self-explanatory. Whilst male ejaculate was known, its makeup, at microscopic levels, was not. Written some fourteen hundred years ago, it pre dates the ability of humans to see these things, or to understand the clinical process, by some thirteen centuries. Admittedly, the way in which the event is described, can only be described as poetic and simplistic, but considering the time in which it was written, it is an astoundingly accurate description.

This is just one of many instances where the writings in various Holy Scriptures explain in their own inimitable way, what the scientists of recent decades have struggled to discover. Why can't the various schools of thought in the various religions and disciplines of science come to an understanding? '*A rose by another name would smell as sweet.'* Like the Abrahamic religions that fight and dispute each other's claims to authenticity. Can't they see that it's all the same story, the same world, the same life?

The description of the Creation in the Holy Bible, and the description of conception in the Holy Qur'an, both highlight the fact that these people, somehow, had been informed. Neither case can be attributed to race memory by means of folk tales, as both have only been proven by science in the past century. How can the multiplicity of accurate descriptions of a seventh century prophet be put aside as coincidence? I think that a serious and open minded study of the scriptures by those who purport to be the academics of today would lead to a few new avenues of investigation, and possibly show the way to some answers to the questions we all ask.

Leaving Africa, 80,000 years ago by way of the Arabian Peninsula, the early H.s.sapiens found the Nile Valley, the Levant and Iraq. They made their first settlements there. There was plenty of water, good climate and hunting and fertile ground that inspired the Agricultural Revolution. It's here that the early folk tales would be re told around fires on balmy evenings; when stomachs were full and the mood was pleasant. They would be classics, tales of men of old that walked tall and proud. Tales of the Paradise that Men had left behind, where all you needed was available just by stretching out your hand....

These stories would, in the absence of writing, be passed on by word of mouth through the generations to the Biblical scribes. Unable to be certain of the exact location of the places described in the stories, they made educated guesses. They were, after all, writing the history of the world, and the world as *they* knew it, was, unfortunately, somewhat different to the world that their forebears, the originators of the tales, would have known it. So are legends born and propagated.

A much more contentious issue than the actual origins of the species is the actual method by which we emerged from the fauna of The Dark Continent. Debates still rage amongst the specialists as to whether we are descendants of one sub species or another. Forget Apes. Our branch of the animal kingdom separated from theirs a good 7 million years ago and from monkeys about 35 million years ago.

I was chatting about the subject with a young friend of mine one day, and much to my surprise, when I said that we are definitely a primate, she glared at me and told me in no uncertain terms that there was no way on Earth that we were descended from monkeys. She was a confirmed (Islamic) follower of Adam and Eve. I never expected to find such a firm belief in religious writings in one so young in our Western Society. She's not uneducated either, heading off to University next year. The incident demonstrated to me just how strong the belief of individuals can be, even in those whom you least expect it; and just how common place those feelings are.

There have been numerous sub species of humans since our branch of the primate tree grew away from the others. It has divided many times since Sahelanthropus tchadensis first graced the face of the Earth. We could have evolved from any one of them. Yet there is no proof as to which one it may have been, if indeed there was one. Just to clarify the point, we are NOT <descended from monkey's> we share a joint ancestor with the other primates. Not quite the same thing.

In a climate that is as unpredictable and as hostile as ours, without some form of personal protection men die very quickly from the cold. Or heat. You become unable to carry on with the sophisticated living and industry that builds space craft and trains astronauts. All your time is spent keeping warm/cool and fending off nature. Life soon descends to the level of basic subsistence. Ask anyone who has been lost in the desert, or jungle; been marooned on an island or cast adrift at sea. Even if books and other items of sophisticated living are at hand, they soon become cannibalised for use in some other basic requirement.

No. Unless there is an abundance of food and protection from the environment, mankind is deprived of the opportunity to utilise his amazing powers of reasoning and imagination.

Conversely, the further he is removed from the savagery of nature, then the more he indulges in art, literature and science. Take for example, the jungle tribes of South America or Papua New Guinea. As naked as the day they were born and many of them still using the Stone Age tools that the rest of us discarded 6,000 years ago. It's not just a coincidence that the colder climates with their clothes wearing inhabitants spawned the Industrial Revolution and modern technology, it was all part of a survival strategy.

God & Mammon

Unfortunately, we've wasted the brainpower we've developed over the millennia by spending most of its time and effort in pursuit of, as the Christian might say, 'worldly goods' or in an Islamic tone, 'dounier'. Money and worldly goods may have their role to play in our society, but they should be treated with wariness. The pursuit of wealth can be damaging far and away beyond that incurred by the individual as greed wreaks havoc in their lives.

Holy Bible (King James Ver.) Mathew 19:23 – 26

19:23 Then said Jesus unto his disciples, Verily I say unto you, That a rich man shall hardly enter into the kingdom of heaven.

19:24 And again I say unto you, It is easier for a camel to go through the eye of a needle, than for a rich man to enter into the kingdom of God.

19:25 When his disciples heard it, they were exceedingly amazed, saying, Who then can be saved?

19:26 But Jesus beheld them, and said unto them, With men this is impossible; but with God all things are possible.

One of the most beautiful and profound pieces of philosophy ever written comes from the New Testament.

Holy Bible (King James Version) Mathew 6:24-29

6:24 No man can serve two masters: for either he will hate the one, and love the other; or else he will hold to the one, and despise the other. Ye cannot serve God and mammon.

6:25 Therefore I say unto you, Take no thought for your life, what ye shall eat, or what ye shall drink; nor yet for your body, what ye shall put on. Is not the life more than meat, and the body than raiment?

6:26 Behold the fowls of the air: for they sow not, neither do they reap, nor gather into barns; yet your heavenly Father feedeth them. Are ye not much better than they?

6:27 Which of you by taking thought can add one cubit unto his stature?

6:28 And why take ye thought for raiment? <u>Consider the lilies of the field, how they grow; they toil not, neither do they spin:</u>

<u>6:29 And yet I say unto you, That even Solomon in all his glory was not arrayed like one of these.</u>

The bankers and financiers that spend all their time 'creating wealth' have totally forgotten about the camel and the eye of the needle. They will end up as the richest men in the graveyard, having impoverished countless millions in the meantime and contributed enormously to Global Warming and climate change. Better surely, to spend a little time appreciating the treasures of this world and the people in it, than to bury yourself in an office and live a life full of stress and to die of some stress related condition.

Industrialists who exploit the natural resources of the planet are the frontline warriors in the war against our environment. The stripping out of huge tracts of rain forest not only deprives other species of their home, but it also diminishes the ability of our biosphere to renew itself and to sustain our food sources, and ultimately us. Then of course there are the by-products of the industrial processes. Not only are huge amounts of pollutants released into water courses and ultimately the oceans, but vast amounts of greenhouse gasses are released into the atmosphere bringing about Global Warming.

The result of this profligate extravagance is, according to the Intergovernmental Panel on Climate Change, that the 'Blue Planet' is now destined to become the 'The Raging Planet', and we and it are all going down the toilet. By now I don't suppose you'll be surprised to hear that the scriptures told us that too.

Holy Bible (King James Version) Michah 7:13

7:13 Notwithstanding the land shall be desolate for them that dwell therein, because of the fruit of their doings.

No ambiguity there then. It all seems to be pretty straight forward to me. Climate change and deforestation are already beginning to affect the productivity of many areas of food production and fisheries and the situation is getting worse, despite a lot of talking going on about how to change things for the better. Water usage in many countries is at an unsustainable level holding the prospect of conflict between countries (some of which have nuclear weapons) who share rivers which are their only source of drinking water. Obviously water shortages lead to a reduction of agriculture and then to food shortages.

We in the affluent countries tend to forget that most of the world's population is living below the poverty line, have no clean water and often no food, never mind education and healthcare. We forget that every day around the world, thousands of children die of diseases which in our richer societies have been eradicated, or can be cured quickly and easily.

In 2016, 15,000 children under five died every day (totaling 5.6 million a year). While a substantial reduction from the 35,000 deaths a day in 1990 (12.6 million a year) it is a terrible reflection of the lack of care we as a species, give each other.

In these days of Global Warming, it doesn't hurt to contemplate this three thousand year old warning. The Holy Qur'an also entreats men to avoid a fixation with what it calls 'dounier' or 'worldly goods'. It's a common theme in the Abrahamic religions, and it would seem to be there for good reason. We have ignored it, and it looks as though we will pay the ultimate price for doing so.

Nothing is new. 70,000 years ago when Toba devastated the planet, it was the hardened few who were used to hardship and deprivation that managed to survive and repopulate the Earth. So it will be again. Millions of people have no house, only the clothes they stand up in, and no hope. The only bright light on their horizon is that when global warming begins to kill the human population by the millions, it is these practiced survivors that will eventually 'Inherit the World'.

I wish them and their descendants every success. May they blossom and prosper and learn from our catastrophic mistakes.

Discounting the Impossible

As magical and mystical properties have featured nowhere in our history, only hard physical facts; we must accept that the reason for our existence is just that, a hard physical fact. No benevolent be-whiskered old gentleman floating on a cloud looking down and giving a helping hand when it was needed. No magical happenings, no artefacts popping into existence from nowhere, just hard, explainable facts. Just like the rest of the Universe. There is no evidence for anything else.

All the facts, all the evidence, point to a well ordered and fabulously engineered system. The Laws of Physics are far too rigid, all-encompassing and predictable to allow any notion that the whole of the Universe came out of chaos. Such well-defined order does not evolve from chaos. It just could not have been created by a happy accident coming out of nothing, as the Big Bang Theory states. It is also equally obvious that just saying "Let there be Light" would be insufficient to produce said item.

Wasn't it the fictional Sherlock Holmes who said,

"Once you have discounted the impossible, whatever is left, however improbable, must be the truth."?

Please point out to me anything that you have personally encountered that was not manufactured, or had parentage. Everything from the largest sun, to the tiniest particle, came from somewhere. There are no exceptions. Which brings us to a rather fascinating conclusion, don't you think? We have to call it "Creation". The evidence dictates that.

There seems to be just too much evidence pointing to an intelligence of some sort or other behind the whole set up. I can see the unmistakable hand of reason at work. Whose hand that is, I leave to your imagination, or your cultural upbringing my dear reader. I freely admit that I am neither scientist nor theologian. More of a philosopher, and then I probably flatter myself.

Many academics and philosophers think that there was an intellectual revolution somewhere in our distant past, somewhere about 50,000 years ago. Why this happened they cannot say, but it is fairly apparent they are correct. Somehow, at some time, something switched on in our brains and took us forward intellectually in a 'quantum leap'. Was it simply genetic? It didn't happen to the other sub species over millions of years, so why should it happen to us? Or was it something else? Are we the intellectual and spiritual beings we are because of Divine Intervention? Was the earthly body of the humble Hominin taken by a greater power and instilled with an intelligence and imagination that would bring us to where we are today? Having considered the evidence presented so far, I don't think it seems as impossible as it did before. Something tells me you have an opinion about that. OK, but, *whatever* it is, as my old Dad used to say,

'I might not agree with what you say, but I would defend to the death your right to (politely) *say it'*.

DNA research has yet to pinpoint the Hominin sub species we came from, if, as I say, we came from any of them. It's more likely that we are the result of a cross breeding of species, a hybrid, possibly with a mutation in the DNA recombination.

On the other hand, who's to say that the mating of the individuals concerned and the intellect it spawned wasn't by Divine Inspiration?

After all, aren't all good marriages, 'Made in Heaven'?

Many and varied are the stories from the scriptures. They are mainly confined to the Old Testament as the Holy Qur'an is narrated from an entirely different perspective. There are a few stories from the Islamic traditions though, but they are just that, stories, parables used to entertain and educate. The Bible though, is the source of many mysterious tales, everything from the disappearance of the Ark of the Covenant to the fabulous Mines of Solomon. We take a look at some of the Bible stories and see if we can shed a little light on them, and then, we can read some of the tales from the Islamic tradition.

Moses & the Mountain of God

If ever a man pushed his luck, surely it must have been Moses. Right from the start, at just a few days old, he is living on the edge. An infant refugee from the wrath of Pharaoh, Moses is set adrift on the crocodile infested waters of the Nile. We could guess here that his Guardian Angel was keeping him for something special!

Just in case you don't know it, here's a shortened version of the story of how baby Moses was set adrift in a woven basket on the river Nile by his desperate slave mother. (Exodus 2:1) He was found and rescued by the daughter of the Pharaoh. He was then raised as her son in the royal household and eventually became a senior member of the ruling class. One day he kills a slave overseer (Exodus 2:12) for beating a Hebrew slave, and flees Egypt in fear of his life.

Let's pick up the story in Midian, where Moses has gone to escape prosecution as a murderer. He is sitting next to a well when some local girls bring their sheep to drink, but other shepherds, men, chase them away so their sheep can drink first. Moses won't have this though. Not being used to bad behaviour, and being very used to getting his own way, he tears a strip off the bullying lads and chases them and their sheep away. A lifetime of the country's best food in the palace, and military training by Egypt's finest would have given Moses a decided advantage in most fights. Moses tells the girls to carry on watering their flock and helps them do it. When the girls tell their father, Jethro, (described as the 'Priest of Midian') what happened, he insists that they bring Moses to their tent and that he shares a meal with them.

The upshot of this is that Moses stays there, marries one of the daughters, (Zipporah) and takes over the job of shepherd. Midianites are also mentioned in the Holy Qur'an.

Sura al-Qasas 28:22-24

22.And as he made his way towards Midian, he said, "I trust my Lord will guide me to the right way."

23.When he arrived at the well of Midian, he found a group of people watering their herds. Apart from them, he noticed two women holding back their herd. He asked them, "What is the problem?" They replied, "We cannot water our animals until the other shepherds are done, for our father is a very old man."

24.So he watered their herd for them, then withdrew to the shade and prayed, "My Lord! I am truly in desperate need of whatever provision You may have in store for me."

It is also described in Exodus.

Holy Bible (King James Version) Exodus 2:15-21

[15] *Now when Pharaoh heard this thing, he sought to slay Moses. But Moses fled from the face of Pharaoh, and dwelt in the land of Midian: and he sat down by a well.*

[16] *Now the priest of Midian had seven daughters: and they came and drew water, and filled the troughs to water their father's flock.*

[17] *And the shepherds came and drove them away: but Moses stood up and helped them, and watered their flock.*

[18] *And when they came to Reuel their father, he said, How is it that ye are come so soon to day?*

[19] *And they said, An Egyptian delivered us out of the hand of the shepherds, and also drew water enough for us, and watered the flock.*

[20] *And he said unto his daughters, And where is he? why is it that ye have left the man? call him, that he may eat bread.*

[21] *And Moses was content to dwell with the man: and he gave Moses Zipporah his daughter.*

First of all we need to locate this Land of Midian. The Midianites were nomadic people and migrated from NW Saudi Arabia as far north as the southern Levant. William Dever (Professor of Near Eastern Archaeology & Anthropology University of Arizona) was of the opinion that Midian was in the "northwest Arabian Peninsula, on the east shore of the Gulf of Aqaba on the Red Sea". However, a nomadic people by their very nature cannot be identified with a static geographical point.

Midian is also a place where that beloved item of all archaeologists, pottery, was made in the Bronze Age. It is known as Qurayyah Painted Ware (QPW). We know it was used by the Midianites because it is found in its largest quantities at sites in the southern Levant, especially Timna. According to Professor Beno Rothenberg: (founder of the Institute for Archaeological Metallurgical Studies, University College London) A temple built for Egyptian miners in Timna, (just north of Eilat in Israel) was taken over by the Midianites after it was abandoned and filled with, amongst other things, QPW pottery, proof positive that the Midianites moved further north than Eilat.

So we now know they travelled from Qurayyah to Timna. Did they go anywhere else on the migrations? In the Book of Judges, there is the story of Gideon lying in wait for the Midianites.

*Judges 7:24 "Come down against the Midianites and seize the waters of the Jordan **ahead of them** as far as **Beth Barah."***

This shows the Midianites migrated as far as Beth Barah, a few miles east of Jericho. Gideon's warriors are instructed to wait ahead of them, which infers that the Midianites were moving northwards. So we now have conclusive evidence of at least part of their migration route. It goes from Qurayyah, via Timna and at least as far north as Beth Barah. This indicates that they followed the River Jordan. Quite logical for nomadic shepherds if you think about it.

So we have Moses living with the Midianite family of Jethro, married to Zipporah and looking after the sheep or goats or whatever. Must have been annoying for the other shepherds! Might have been able to cut in front of girls and an old man at the well, but now they have to wait for Moses to finish. That's Karma for you!

All this leaves us facing the fact that Moses was shepherding somewhere along the Qurayyah-Timna-Beth Barah route when he saw the Burning Bush on some mountain and was instructed by God to bring the Children of Israel out of bondage in Egypt.

Holy Bible (King James Version) Exodus 3:1

3:1 Now Moses kept the flock of Jethro his father in law, the priest of Midian: and he led the flock to the backside of the desert, and came to the mountain of God, even to Horeb.

3:2 And the angel of the LORD appeared unto him in a flame of fire out of the midst of a bush; and he looked, and, behold, the bush burned with fire, and the bush was not consumed.

The Hebrew word that is translated into the English King James Bible as bush is seneh (סנה), which refers in particular to brambles. Seneh, only appears in two places in the Bible, both of which describe the burning bush. It is possible that the reference to a burning bush is based on a mistaken interpretation of Sinai (סיני), a mountain described in Exodus 19:18 as being on fire. Another possibility is that the use of seneh (סנה) may be a deliberate pun on Sinai (סיני), a feature common in Hebrew texts.

As for Horeb, well, the location of Horeb is disputed. Jewish and Christian scholars have advanced varying opinions as to its whereabouts since biblical times. Elijah is described in 1st Book of Kings 19:1–21 as traveling to Horeb from Beer Sheba in a way which implies that its position was familiar when that was written, but there are no biblical references set any later in time. Additionally the passage identifies a cave large enough to lodge in, which can be found on Mt Sinai. However, there was, apparently a cave on the Mountain of God, as Jeremiah hid the tabernacle and the Ark of the Covenant in a **cave** there much later, according to the 2nd Book of Maccabees (a book in the part of the Bible known as the Apocrypha).

Holy Bible (King James Version) 2nd Maccabees 2:4-5

2:4 It was also contained in the same writing, that the prophet being warned of God, commanded the Tabernacle and the Arke to goe with him, as he went up the mountaine where Moises climed up, and sawe the heritage of God.

2:5 and when Jeremie came thither, he found an hollow cave wherein he laid the Tabernacle and the Arke, and the altar of incense, & so stopped the doore.

Remember, Moses was obviously not too far from his father in law's tent as he was tending the family flock somewhere along the Midianites nomadic route. He certainly wouldn't be hundreds of kilometres from home up a barren mountain range in Egypt. The descriptions we have got of the Mountain of God certainly fit Mt Sinai, but they also fit another mountain, one which is right on the Midianites migration route.

Holy Bible (King James Version) Exodus 3:11-12

3:11 And Moses said unto God, Who am I, that I should go unto Pharaoh, and that I should bring forth the children of Israel out of Egypt?

3:12 And he said, Certainly I will be with thee; and this shall be a token unto thee, that I have sent thee: <u>When thou hast brought forth the people out of Egypt, ye shall serve God upon this mountain.</u>

This is the million dollar piece of evidence. Moses will bring the Israelites out of Egypt and then serve God on the same mountain. The next time we see Moses communing with God on a mountain, he is being given the Law, the Ten Commandments (there are actually many more!) and the time after that he is being shown the Promised Land. This is all done on God's Mountain; a mountain chosen by God to deliver the Law, to show Moses the Promised Land, and to have the Tabernacle and the Ark of the Covenant returned to Him. Surely no other mountain is more qualified to be called the Mountain of God? My contention is that all this took place on Mount Nebo, the mountain that is on the Midianites migration route and which overlooks the Jordan Valley and the land we know today as Israel.

So there we have it; the real location of the Mountain of God, and also the last known resting place of the Ark of the Covenant. It is the same mountain that Moses died on and was buried next to 'in the valley' by the very hand of God himself.

It makes a great deal of sense, if you think about it, for the same mountain to feature in all of these events. The name 'The Mountain of God' implies that there is only one. We never hear of 'The <u>Mountains</u> of God'. So if there is a sacred mountain, then surely the aforementioned events would all take place upon it.

Today Mount Nebo is the site of a Franciscan monastery and a site of pilgrimage and tourism. It is well worth a visit.

Nebo, was the name of a major god in the Assyrian-Babylonian religions, and the mountain we are talking about was considered to be his home. It may be just coincidence, but it could also indicate that Yahweh, the god of the Israelites was also known to other peoples.

Nebo, incidentally, was the Mesopotamian god of literacy, the rational arts, scribes and wisdom.

Mount Nebo is far from the Red Sea coast and the Sinai desert, and a very long way indeed from the place of Christian tradition where Moses is supposed to have been given the Law, Mount Sinai (Jebel Musa).

Ask yourself, what would a Midianite shepherd be doing hundreds of kilometres from his traditional grazing grounds, in the middle of a desert mountain range? Bear in mind that it is impossible to see the Jordan Valley and the Promised Land from Mount Sinai, and if you were a shepherd, the mountains of the Sinai desert would be the very last place you'd take your sheep. No grazing for sheep whatsoever.

A local man told me that his father once knew an old man who remembered when it last rained there. Probably just a good line for a tourist, but you get his point? Temperatures range from as high as a skin blistering 50c during the day, to a bone chilling -3c at night. As you curl up in your tent at night you can sometimes hear rocks splitting apart due to the rapid change in temperature.

Location of the Mountain of God

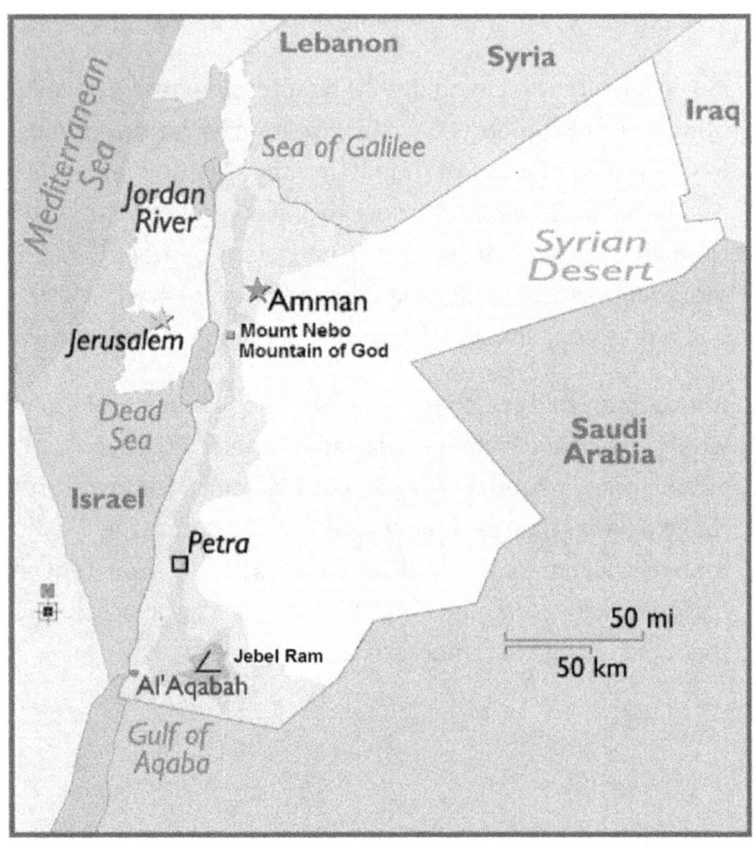

Moses Divides the Red Sea

Hollywood really went to town on this one. Big screen images of Charlton Heston as Moses standing on a rock, arms held aloft and the mighty deep parting before him. Not far behind him, Yul Brynner as Ramses leading the vast Egyptian army to destruction. Great stuff, classic cinema.

So impressive was Cecil B. De Mille's 1956 Oscar winning movie, 'The Ten Commandments' that for many people, it, not the story in the Bible, defined what happened to Moses and the Israelites. As in Hollywood, Exodus has a bit of a problem with the details.

The Red Sea is the northern tip of the African Great Rift Valley. It splits in two at Ras Mohammed, dividing Egypt with the Gulf of Suez, and separating Saudi Arabia and the Sinai with the Gulf of Aqaba. This particular rift continues north east, providing a home for the Dead Sea, the Jordan River, and Lake Tiberius, known in Biblical times as the Sea of Galilee.

 If Moses did indeed part the Red Sea, his entourage would have had to be rather surefooted to cross it. In some places, this narrow sea is 2000 feet (700 metres) deep, with vertical walls that drop down to the bottom. I've dived there. I've seen them. It resembles the Grand Canyon filled with water. Not a practical proposition for a mountaineer, let alone for women, children and the old folks. We will have to look elsewhere to find a suitable crossing point.

Holy Bible (King James Version) 14:19-22

14:19 And the angel of God, which went before the camp of Israel, removed and went behind them; and the pillar of the cloud went from before their face, and stood behind them:

14:20 And it came between the camp of the Egyptians and the camp of Israel; and it was a cloud and darkness to them, but it gave light by night to these: so that the one came not near the other all the night.

14:21 And Moses stretched out his hand over the sea; and the LORD caused the sea to go back by a strong east wind all that night, and made the sea dry land, and the waters were divided.

14:22 And the children of Israel went into the midst of the sea upon the dry ground: and the waters were a wall unto them on their right hand, and on their left.

How about this pillar of cloud that was in front of them to start with, but was behind them when they crossed the 'sea'? Three thousand six hundred years ago the volcano known as Santorini, or Thera, erupted in the Aegean Sea. It was the largest eruption in recorded history, and probably second only to Toba in Human history. You can still see (as with Toba) the remains of the caldera (crater) today. It measures about 12 by 7 km (7.5 by 4.5 miles), and is surrounded by 300 m (980 feet) high, steep cliffs on three sides. It forms a lagoon some 400 metres deep and ocean liners sometimes cruise through it. When it erupted the column of ash would have risen many kilometres into the air, and ash from it circled the globe. There is evidence that it affected the climate and crops, as far away as China. It would have been discernible from Egypt without much problem. Thera decided to wreak its particular form of havoc just at the same time, or thereabouts, as the Israelites were abandoning the Pharaoh.

If it was at the same time, Moses and his people would have seen the cloud of ash to the north west of them (in front) as they travelled up from, presumably Pithom, which was somewhere in the vicinity of Cairo. They would have then turned east, having travelled far enough north to pass around the Red Sea. This would have been a much more logical route than heading directly for the Red Sea and all the difficulties of moving a mass of people across it. The ash cloud would now have been more or less behind them, as they headed for the Nile Delta crossings into Sinai. I wonder, could the glow from the distant eruption also have been seen at night too, accounting for the 'pillar of fire' at night?

They are now heading across the Nile Delta. At some point in its eruption, Santorini is known to have caused a massive tsunami, which could easily have reached Egypt. If the tsunami caused the water in the Delta to retreat, a usual precursor to a tsunami, then Moses would have had his 'parting of the waters'. Having crossed the Delta, Moses would have seen the pursuing army being engulfed by the wave as it travelled inland. No doubt, to desert people, this scene would have been nothing less than miraculous, and in their situation, a real God send. A huge wave so far inland

and taking the threatening soldiers with it would have been Divine intervention indeed.

King Solomon's Mines and the Queen of Sheba.

One of the legendary figures in the Old Testament and as mysterious as any woman could wish to be, the Queen of Sheba must rate as an all-time Super Celeb. Along with that other ancient, but well documented female celebrity, Cleopatra; this monarch of old has featured in many tales and much folklore. Known to the Ethiopian people as 'Makeda' or 'Maqueda' this queen has been called a variety of names by different peoples in different times. To King Solomon of Israel she was the 'Queen of Sheba'. In Islamic tradition she was called 'Balqis' or 'Balkis' by the Arabians, who say she came from the city of Sheba, also called Mareb, in Yemen. It is generally thought that she ruled over both Yemen and Ethiopia. The Roman historian Josephus calls her 'Nicaule'.

She is thought to have been born on January 5, in the 10th century BC. Legend has it that she brought spices, red sandal wood and some four and a half tons of gold as a gift 'fit for a King' from her homeland when she visited King Solomon 'to witness his wisdom and majesty.' That must make her one of the richest females in history, second only to Cleopatra; a welcome visitor indeed at the Court of Solomon.

There are many tales about the Queen of Sheba. She was said to have been seduced by Solomon, and went home pregnant with his son. This child is known by various names. His mother named him Ibn al-Hakim, "son of the wise man." Some Jewish, Islamic and Persian sources claim that this child was Nebuchadnezzar. Ethiopians believe him to be David II (the name given him by Solomon), who later called himself Menelek, and who was the first king of the Ethiopian dynasty.

The Islamic versions of the story have her marrying Solomon, and that she returns to her country and decrees that from thence forth Islam shall be the only religion of the people.

Legend has it that she was Queen of a land famous for its gold mines, and that these mines became known as 'King Solomon's Mines' because they were the source of his wealth. With four tons of gold as a gift from the Queen of Sheba, a good part of his wealth would indeed have originated here.

The name of this land was recorded in the Bible as Ophir, but there is no country or province with this name today. However, in Eritrea, in the horn of Africa is the land of the Afari people. This area is known as Afar. It is the area in which the fossil remains of many ancient Hominins have been found, notably the remains of a female Australopithecus afarensis, popularly known as 'Lucy'. As in many other cases the phonetics of a name give an insight to its history. From Ophir to Afar is only a minor step of accent. It would seem that she was indeed the Queen of Afar, giving her access to the gold mines and mineral wealth of Africa as well as the highly sought after incense of Yemen.

King Solomon was said to have received a gift every three years from Ophir as a tribute. John Masefield, says in his poem "Cargoes"

Quinquireme of Nineveh from distant Ophir,
Rowing home to haven in sunny Palestine,
With a cargo of ivory, And apes and peacocks,
Sandalwood, cedar wood, and sweet white wine.

Visiting Ethiopia today you will find many gold mining sites, which local people operate in a manner which is known to have been used for at least three thousand years in the Middle East. Upper Egypt, or Nubia, which borders this area, was the source of most of the Pharaohs gold.

The Queen of Sheba also held the title 'Queen of Ethiopia and of Egypt', and ruling Yemen as well, she must have been a powerful ruler who was quite accustomed to living with wealth and opulence. Girl Power isn't just a 20th Century phenomenon.

Noah and the Flood

Here we have a story that is common to many cultures around the world and not just to those in and around the Middle East. The North American Indians have a whole host of stories relating to watery catastrophes. One of them, from the Cascade Mountains tells of a time when a flood covered the land. It tells of an old man and his family, who, seeking refuge on a raft was blown by the wind to a certain mountain. He stayed there and sent a crow to search for land, but it returned without finding any. Sometime later he sent it off again, and this time it brought back a leaf and the old man knew the water was receding.

There are obvious similarities here to the Biblical account of the Flood. In the Bible, Noah sends a dove. In various North American Indian accounts the bird is a pigeon, a crow a duck and a kingfisher. Intriguingly, all these accounts of floods predate the arrival of the Christian religion in North America. Conversely, the accounts of Noah and the flood were written thousands of years before Columbus sailed to the New World.

Floods of course, are pretty commonplace, and most communities will have suffered from them at some time in their history, but none are so well known as Noah and his particular inundation. The writers of Genesis seem to be relating an incident that is recorded elsewhere in the annals of the ancient world. Dare I even suggest that they may have 'borrowed' their tale of watery catastrophe from The Epic of Gilgamesh (Tablet 11)? This tells of a very similar occurrence and of Gilgamesh building a huge boat, in which he and his family along with other creatures escape the deluge.

Just as dawn began to glow there arose from the horizon a black cloud. Adad rumbled inside of it, before him went Shullat and Hanish, heralds going over mountain and land. Erragal pulled out the mooring poles, forth went Ninurta and made the dikes overflow. The Anunnaki lifted up the* *torches, setting the land ablaze with their flare. Stunned shock over Adad's deeds overtook the heavens, and turned to blackness all that had been light.*

The... land shattered like a... pot. All day long the South Wind blew..., blowing fast, submerging the mountain in water, overwhelming the people like an attack. No one could see his fellow, they could not recognize each other in the torrent. The gods were frightened by the Flood, and retreated, ascending to the heaven of Anu.

A fifth day, a sixth, Mount Nimush held the boat, allowing no sway. When a seventh day arrived I sent forth a dove and released it. The dove went off, but came back to me; no perch was visible so it circled back to me. I sent forth a swallow and released it. The swallow went off, but came back to me; no perch was visible so it circled back to me. I sent forth a raven and released it. The raven went off, and saw the waters slither back. It eats, it scratches, it bobs, but does not circle back to me.

**Adad is the Storm God*

The Epic of Gilgamesh was written about 2500 BCE, some 900 years before the writers of Genesis supposedly undertook their work. So just what happened to inspire all these myths? There are many causes of floods, but the most spectacular are usually caused by earthquakes under bodies of water, or earth slides *into* bodies of water. The resultant displacement of water causes a wave. A tsunami, sometimes incorrectly referred to as a tidal wave. No doubt many of the tales of great floods are telling of tsunamis, but I have a suspicion that Noah's flood may have had another source.

Take a look at a map of Turkey and the surrounding area. Notice anything? The thing that catches my eye is the abundance of lakes in and around the area, and the number of Islands in the Aegean Sea. It actually looks as though the area has been flooded and the water didn't quite finish draining away. That of course is not the case. The lakes are fed by rivers and streams. But the Islands in the Aegean hold a clue here. It's shallow. Some of it is as little as seventeen meters in depth. It wouldn't take much of a drop in sea level to expose quite a lot of land. According to a workshop held at the National Center for Marine Research, Greece, on the topic "Aegean Sea", sponsored by the U.S. Office of Naval Research;

"The Aegean is relatively shallow compared to ocean basins and has many sills, ridges, and islands. In addition, tidal currents are much weaker than in the major ocean basins."

If we go way back in time, some 21,000 years, to the peak of the current glacial period, (which began about 70,000 years ago), we would find that apart from the ice at the poles and the highest mountains that we know, (Himalayas, Andes, etc.) ice in the form of glaciers was pretty commonplace on most mountain ranges. Outside these main ice sheets, and of particular interest to us, widespread glaciation occurred on the Alps, to the east on the Caucasus Mountains and on the mountains of Turkey and Iran. All were capped by local ice fields or small ice sheets. All this ice was, of course, formed by snow, which came from evaporation of the oceans. This had caused the sea levels to drop by some 125 meters, leaving the Northern Aegean substantially shallower and even dry in some parts. The effect this would have on the Black Sea in particular would have been to isolate it from the Mediterranean Sea or at the very least, to have reduced the flow of water between it and the Aegean.

In a series of expeditions from the Woods Hole Oceanographic Institute of Massachusetts, a team of marine archeologists led by Dr. Robert Ballard, (Professor of Oceanography at the University of Rhode Island), identified what appeared to be ancient shorelines, freshwater snail shells, drowned river valleys, tool-worked timbers, and man-made structures in roughly 100 meters (330 feet) of water off the Black Sea coast of modern Turkey. Although radiocarbon dating of freshwater mollusk remains indicated an age of about 7,500 years, the actual date that they were living is not certain, as this particular method of dating can be quite inaccurate. Even so, it seems that about 10,000 years ago, there was no sea water in the Black Sea. It was a fresh water lake.

Some experts claim that the flow of water into the Black Sea stopped altogether. As the big freeze continued, evaporation would have lowered the level of the black Sea, until the 'big melt' started, about 12,500 years ago. Once this got underway the result would have been a reversal of the whole process. Sea levels rose, dried up ancient rivers refilled, and the oceans began to rise as the melting glaciers and ice sheets drained into them. The warmer climate also meant more rain as opposed to snow, and so 'liquid' precipitation increased. More rain, bigger rivers, higher seas.

At some point, the rising Aegean filled the Sea of Marmora, and then probably overtopped the narrow strip of land that joins Europe to Anatolia. This would be the creation of the Bosporus as we know it today. This influx of sea water killed off the freshwater life, and brought about very dramatic rise in the level of the Black Sea. In fact, it is thought that the daily flow was something like 200 times the amount of water that goes over Niagara Falls each day.

Just a minute, are we getting into tabloid territory here? You know, comparisons of things being as long as football pitches and as heavy as a certain number of jumbo jets? I'll give it to you in real terms. About 160 million cubic meters a day goes over Niagara Falls. So the flow into the Black Sea would have been about 320 billion cubic meters a day. 320 cubic kilometers. That's a HUGE amount of water.

Let's paint a picture of the scene. Mr. H. Sapiens is sitting on a (Turkish Black Sea) beach with his wife and kids. They are, according to Prof. Robert Ballard, some 100 meters below the present level of the Black Sea.

One of the kids points out a trickle of water running from the top of the beach. It increases rapidly from a trickle to a worrying river. They move away, along the beach, but very soon the river has become a torrent as the water cuts away a channel for itself. As the channel widens, the family have to run along the beach to escape the ever widening rapids. Dad is pretty streetwise and so leads his family up to higher ground, up the beach away from the water. As the days pass he watches as the rapids become a massive torrent, and he has to lead his family, along with the rest of his tribe, way down the shoreline to get away from it. The noise has increased to a deafening roar. The level of their fresh water lake is rising fast and they have to climb to ever higher ground.

For weeks the water rises, inundating many miles of what used to be their hunting grounds. Their villages are drowned, whole communities swept away along with their animals. When everything settles down again, thousands of people are gone along with their main source of fresh water. The whole of the landscape has been transformed. It's a whole new world.

No wonder that the story became a folk tale. About a hundred generations later, the story was written down, to be wondered at and about for the rest of time. Just how much truth there is in the story of Noah, we can never say. But as stories go, it's a good one, the big boat, the animals. The children's song says that 'The animals went in two by two, the Elephant and the Kangaroo...' (Kangaroo?) You can even see the Jewish element in the story.

Holy Bible (King James Version) Genesis 6:19-7:3

6:19 And of every living thing of all flesh, two of every sort shalt thou bring into the ark, to keep them alive with thee; they shall be male and female.

6:20 Of fowls after their kind, and of cattle after their kind, of every creeping thing of the earth after his kind, two of every sort shall come unto thee, to keep them alive.

6:21 And take thou unto thee of all food that is eaten, and thou shalt gather it to thee; and it shall be for food for thee, and for them.

That's the 'two by two'.   Now we come to the Kosher bit.

6:22 Thus did Noah; according to all that God commanded him, so did he.

7:1 And the LORD said unto Noah, Come thou and all thy house into the ark; for thee have I seen righteous before me in this generation.

7:2 <u>Of every clean beast thou shalt take to thee by sevens</u>, the male and his female: and of beasts that are not clean by two, the male and his female.

7:3 Of fowls also of the air by sevens, the male and the female; to keep seed alive upon the face of all the earth.

Jews can't eat what Jewish Law regards as 'unclean.' Only those things that are 'clean'. Pigs, for example, are famously 'unclean'. Poultry ('birds of the air') are clean, and can be eaten. So, sensibly, take seven of those. Five to eat, two to breed. There's no point in wasting room on more than two if you can't eat them. Though they didn't know it at the time, according to Archbishop Usher, Noah and his kin had to survive for twenty one weeks and three days, until the seventeenth of July, 600 BC, so food would have been a bit tight, so to speak.

I reckon the Dove had a narrow escape, and just how did Noah get his hands on some Kangaroos?

12 FROM THE ISLAMIC TRADITION

The Holy Qur'an takes a different perspective to the Holy Bible, so I am including some of the better known anecdotes that are popular with Muslims.

King Solomon & the Ant

Once there was a big famine in Palestine. It was during the time of the Prophet, Prophet Suleiman (King Solomon). He came out with his people and proceeded to an open place in the desert to pray for the rains to come. Suddenly, he saw an ant standing on two legs, raising its hands up towards the sky and saying,

Oh Allah! We are but very small among all Thy creatures. We cannot survive without Thy grace. Please bestow upon us Thy sustenance and do not punish us because of the sins of human beings. Please send down the rains so that trees can grow, farms become green and grains become available and we have our food to eat."

Prophet Suleiman knew the language of all animals. He told his people,

"Let us go home. The prayer of this ant is enough." It then rained heavily and all the land became green and productive.

This just goes to prove that no matter how small your voice, it can count, so I'll continue writing.

The Holy Qur'an 17:61-65 (Children of Israel)

And when We (Allah) said to the angels, 'Fall down prostrate before Adam ', they fell prostrate except Iblis (Satan) who said,

'Shall I bow down before him whom You have created of clay? Do you see this creature whom You have honoured above me? If You give me grace until the Day of Resurrection, I will certainly destroy his offspring, save but a few'.

'Be gone!' said He. 'But you and whoever of them follows you will have Hell for reward. An ample reward it shall be. Rouse with your voice whomever you are able. Muster against them your horse men and your fool men. Be their partner in their wealth and in their off spring. Make them promises. Whatever Satan promises them is only for deceit. But over My true servants you shall have no power. Your Lord is their all Sufficient Guardian.

One of the stories from Islam is how God made the Angels from Light, and made them incapable of doing wrong. He then made Satan out of fire, and made him incapable of doing good. He then made Adam in his own image and gave him the choice between the two. An individual's choices during his lifetime reveal whether he is a follower of Satan or a follower of the Angels, determining an afterlife in Heaven or in Hell.

Excerpt from the Prophet Mohammad's Last Sermon (7th March 632 CE)

"Beware of Satan, for the safety of your religion. He has lost all hope that he will ever be able to lead you astray in big things, so beware of following him in small things.

O People, it is true that you have certain rights with regard to your women, but they also have rights over you. Remember that you have taken them as wives only under God's trust and with His permission. If they abide by your right then to them belongs the right to be fed and clothed in kindness. Do treat your women well and be kind to them for they are your partners and committed helpers. It is your right that they do not make friends with anyone of whom you do not approve, as well as never to be unchaste.

O People, listen to me in earnest, worship God, say your five daily prayers, fast during the month of Ramadan and give of your wealth in charity. Perform Haj (Pilgrimage to Mecca) if you can afford to.

All mankind is from Adam and Eve*, an Arab has no superiority over a non-Arab, nor a non-Arab over an Arab; also a white has no superiority over a black, nor a black has any superiority over a white, except by piety and good action. Learn that every Muslim is a Brother to every Muslim, and that the Muslims constitute one Brotherhood. Nothing shall be legitimate to a Muslim unless it was given freely and willingly.*

Do not, therefore, do injustice to yourselves."

Despite popular opinion and local traditions, equality between the sexes and races are a fundamental of true Islam.

Planet Earth photographed from Apollo 17

This image was catalogued by Johnson Space Center of the United States National Aeronautics and Space Administration (NASA) under Photo ID: AS17-148-22727.

Well done, NASA

Do You Like Kipling?

1st Man. "Do you like Kipling?"
2nd Man. "I don't know, I've never Kippled...'

Beyond the path of the outmost sun
Through utter darkness hurled,
Further than ever comet flared
or vagrant star dust swirled
Live such as fought and sailed and ruled
and loved and made our world.
Tis theirs to sweep through the ringing deep
Where Azrael's outposts are
Or buffet a path through the Pit's red wrath
When God goes out to war
Or hang with the reckless Seraphim
On the rein of a red maned star.
They take their mirth in the joy of the Earth
They dare not grieve for her pain
They know of toil and the end of toil
They know God's law is plain
So they whistle the Devil to make them sport
Who know that Sin is vain.

Rudyard Kipling

Just thought I'd put this in. I've often Kippled....

We call it home. Earth. Two thirds of its surface is covered by water, and the dry part is inhabited by over seven billion people.

Earth is 4.5 billion years old. It's the third planet from the star we call The Sun. The Sun has a system of planets, and our 'solar system' can be found on the 'Orion' arm of our spiral galaxy, The Milky Way. (see image below) It's a very long way, about 23,000 light years, from the centre of our galaxy, and our galaxy is very long way indeed from the centre of the Universe.

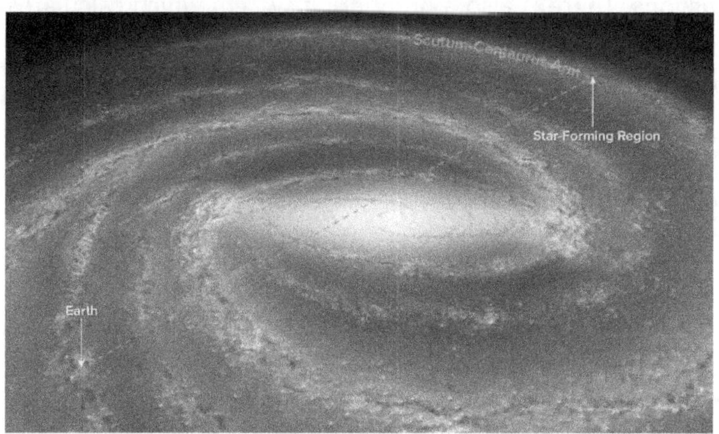

Courtesy of Smithsonian Institute.

So, all things considered, we're not exactly prominent on the galactic stage. In fact if you were an alien trying to find life in this corner of the Universe, you could look for millions of years and still come no-where close to finding our galaxy, never mind our sun. In this context the word 'insignificant' applies.

When we consider the rest of the Universe, we are trying to put into some sort of context facts and figures that we are just not used to recognising. The average person is quite capable of getting a handle on periods of time that are measured in thousands of years. Get into the millions of years and it usually gets a bit vague for most people. Billions of years are something else entirely.

To avoid confusion I'm going to use what is called the 'Short Billion', or 1 with 9 noughts after it. It is One thousand millions. There is also a numbering system which calculates a Billion as a 1 with 12 noughts after it, called a 'Long Billion' which is one million millions, but as scientists, including cosmological astronomers use the short billion, I will too.

When you say "A billion" it doesn't conjure up any particular shape or size does it? Let's try and give it some perspective.   Take the basic measurement of time, a second, sixty in a minute. No problem here, we're all used to them. When you think that there are 3600 seconds in an hour, the numbers start to get a bit unwieldy, but an hour is something we're all familiar with so again no real problem. However, if you start to add the noughts and run up to a million seconds, how long do you think that is? Had a guess? Then here's the answer. Its 11.57 days.

Let's try a billion. That's one thousand times a million, so in this case it would be 11,570 days or….32.7 <u>YEARS</u>. Quite a difference. When you shift from million to billion, it's a huge jump, its far bigger in scale than the jump from a thousand to a million. The incredible fact is that when we come to discuss time and distances in the context of the Universe, even billions are inadequate, they are just too small to be of any real use. What is needed is something that can describe indescribable distance. It's a tough one that, but not impossible.

What we need are Light Years. That's the distance a particle of light (photon) travels in one year. Light has been timed at 186,282.4 mile per second (2990,792,458 metres per second)

Let's just try to give you a perspective on that. *There are 60 seconds in one minute, 3600 seconds in an hour, and 86,400 seconds in a day.* So in one day that particle of light would have travelled: (here we go with the big math's again....) 186,282.4 x 86,400 = 16,094,799,360 miles. The calculator was only just big enough. Just to help you say it: Sixteen billion, ninety four million, seven hundred and ninety nine thousand, three hundred and sixty miles an hour.

It would get to the Moon in 1.2 seconds and to the Sun in eight minutes. To get from one side of the Milky Way to the other would take it about 90,000 years.

That's about 5,878,625,373,183.6 miles which is.........(need a bigger calculator) about five hundred and forty thousand trillion miles.

How many football pitches is that then....?

A 'MATTER' OF PERSPECTIVE

A Cosmologist and a Rabbi were talking.

"Don't give me all that rubbish about God making the Universe!" said the Cosmologist. "You think that there's an old gentleman with a big beard sitting on a cloud somewhere, who created all the matter in the Universe in six days! You're crazy!"

"Oh, yes?" replied the Rabbi. "You say that it all came from nothing out of nowhere. And _you_ call _me_ crazy?"

14 THE (REALLY) BIG BANG.

We have here, one of the most argued about, most controversial topics that never fails to bring the confrontation between the 'Darwinists' and the 'Creationists' to a blistering crescendo.

Fred Hoyle is credited with coining the term *Big Bang* during a 1949 radio broadcast on the BBC. It is reported that Hoyle, who favored the alternative "steady state"* cosmological model, intended this to be pejorative, but he explicitly denied this and said it was just a striking image meant to highlight the difference between the two models. OK. So what is the theory?

The theory that states that the Universe was not made, but has always been here.

The Big Bang theory is a cosmological model that explains the creation of the Universe. According to the Big Bang theory, the Universe was once an extremely hot and dense singularity which expanded rapidly. This rapid expansion caused the young Universe to cool and resulted in its present continuously expanding state. According to the most recent measurements and observations, (2018) this original state existed approximately 13.77 billion years ago, which is considered to be the age of the Universe. After its initial expansion from a singularity, the Universe cooled sufficiently to allow energy to be converted into various materials. It took millions of years for some of these materials to combine and form atoms, the building blocks of matter. The first element produced was hydrogen, along with traces of helium and lithium. Eventually, clouds of hydrogen would coalesce through gravity to form stars, super nova would create planets and gravitational fields would form the whole lot into Galaxies.

I think this may be over simplifying again, but that's a fairly crude but adequate description of how it went. To go into more detail and give better descriptions of the process would necessitate spending a few years at University and then spending a few more years researching cosmology, which would be something of a hindrance to my efforts in writing this book, so I'm just going to take the late Prof. Stephen Hawking's (CH CBE FRS FRSA, director of research at the Centre for Theoretical Cosmology at the University of Cambridge) word for it all.

The Big Bang theory is, apparently, is a totally different explanation of the Creation of The Universe to the one expounded by the religious schools of thought who argue that God created everything out of nothing.

Again, it seems to me that the two theories differ only in the wording, but I find it difficult to believe that in a world that is so physically logical, seemingly intelligent people can come up with such illogical conclusions. The thing I find difficult to believe is that highly educated, dedicated scientists, can base their whole theory on something so illogical as a (monumentally understated) Big Bang happening when there was nothing to explode, and nowhere for the singularity to have come from. Where was the singularity? What was it that made it expand, and why so rapidly? OK, I'm oversimplifying again, I'll grant you that, but there had to be *something* there to cause an event..

Also, why is it that equally intelligent and dedicated scholars in the various fields of religion refuse to acknowledge the obvious truths in the scientist's theory? Surely there can be no one left on the planet who disagrees with the idea that exploding stars create the necessary elements to build new worlds and everything in them? By the way, don't you just love the idea that 'we are all just Stardust'?

If there is anyone who can shake their head in the face of such incontrovertible evidence as supplied by the Hubble telescope and its peers, then you'll probably find that they insist the Earth is flat. (ref. 'The Flat Earth Society) But maybe I'm wrong. As I said earlier, I once knew someone who actually believed that the dinosaurs never existed because they weren't mentioned in her Holy Scriptures, or, as she rightly insisted, in anyone else's.

Based on what we seem to know about the creation of new stars from exploding old stars, why could our whole Universe not have been created by a truly gigantic star exploding, or probably, that the singularity was the 'other side' of a black hole in a different universe.? All the facts fit. And it seems (to me at least) to be a logical explanation. But the big drawback here of course, is that the gigantic star and the other universe would have to have come from somewhere. We're stuck with the chicken or the egg paradox again. But at least it neatly explains *our* Universe's (thirteen and a half billion year) time frame.

We also have to consider the fact that our Universe may not be the first or only one. Prof. Stephen Hawking was an expert on what he called Black Holes; collapsing stars creating an infinitesimally small point of matter with a gravitational density that equalled their original size. The gravitational pull of this 'singularity' draws in more matter and so increases the density. An on-going process that is so strong, even light itself cannot escape the situation, hence the name, 'Black Hole'.

Let's imagine for a moment that a Black Hole isn't just a tiny singularity with an enormous mass. Let's imagine it is a tunnel, an actual hole in the fabric of the Universe, a wormhole leading to another dimension. All the matter drawn in would pass through it and out of the other side. So if a wormhole is caused by a collapsing star, then on the other side of the wormhole, would not it appear that a huge amount of matter suddenly appeared from nowhere? A Big Bang? Could this not also be an explanation of where all the matter in our Universe came from? Unfortunately even if this theory is correct, it still doesn't explain where the matter came from in the first place!

There is also a theory that says that the whole of the Universe as we know it is just a speck of dust at the bottom of a policeman's pocket....

According to the Big Bang theory all the matter in the Universe was created when the initial singularity began to expand and then started to cool. Once the Big Bang has got under way, we see that the result of the heat is the creation of matter, gases and so forth, which, given time, succumbs to the effect of gravity and begins to clump together and form stars. Eventually these become so dense and the heat in them so great that fusion begins and they start to 'burn' in the manner that we are all familiar with. Eventually these stars burn out, explode and scatter dust, gamma rays and particles of all manner of things through space. Again, after a while these particles come together again to form planets and the like.

The sequence of events.

First there is nothing. I mean an absolute nothingness, not even Space or Time, not even the concept of nothing exists, if you see what I mean. Suddenly, and without warning or any sort of precursor, there is a massive and cataclysmic eruption of energy in its purest form, giving off unimaginable quantities of energy that expand into the nothingness and give it a perspective we can now understand. The nothingness has had time introduced into it, (the eruption process has a sequence, so time is suddenly relevant and apparent) so it becomes a quantifiable space, called Space!

All this happened 13.77 billion years ago; which is considered to be the age of the Universe (give or take 20 million years). This expansion of energy, heat and light continued for a very long time. Millions of what we now call years. During that time the energy cooled creating various elements of matter. The first to form were Hydrogen, Helium and Lithium. These reacted to gravitational influences and formed stars, which in turn created Carbon and Oxygen by the fusion processes going on inside them, and then dispersed them during their explosive death throes, Super Novas.

This Universe is *really* big. It's huge beyond imagination. In this inconceivably vast place, what do you think is the most common material? I'll give you a clue. It comprises 75% of *everything that exists.* Here's another clue. Its atomic number, not surprisingly, is 1 (one). It's Hydrogen.

Represented by the symbol H, Hydrogen is the lightest and most abundant chemical element, constituting roughly 75% of the Universe's chemical elemental mass. Stars are mainly composed of hydrogen in its plasma (superheated) state. Naturally occurring elemental hydrogen is relatively rare here on Earth, but in its most common form here on the Blue Planet, it's in water. H_2O .

There has been a lot of debate about how our planet obtained so much of the life supporting stuff, because without water, life (as we know it) cannot exist. Most common amongst the various theories is that water came to earth in the form of icy asteroids and comets just after the planet was formed 4.54 billion years ago. In the vastness of space, where the average temperature is about 2.73 Kelvin, (Absolute zero at 0 K is −273.15 °C (−459.67 °F) water cannot exist in its liquid state, so it exists as ice.

The Big Bang was very, very hot, but dark. Light didn't exist until about 300,000 years later. Think about how much hydrogen must have been created at the time of the Big Bang. Stars are made from it, they are basically huge hydrogen bombs.

A typical galaxy contains hundreds of billions of stars, and there are more than 100 billion galaxies in the observable universe. There are about 200 billion trillion stars in the observable universe. Our sun has a mass (weight) of 2 Nonillion kilograms, or a 2 with 30 zeros behind it. Don't ask me. I just collate the info, but it's about 332,950 times the mass of the Earth. So, multiply the number of stars by the number of galaxies by 2 nonillion kilograms, and you start to get the idea of how much hydrogen had to be produced just to make the stars.

Oh, nearly forgot. Our Sun is a small one. Most of the others are bigger, up to 320 times bigger. Anyway, the numbers involved are impossibly big. To say they are 'astronomical' doesn't actually do them justice! The tabloid press couldn't even *imagine* enough Jumbo Jets to hypothesize about the weights involved, and as for the football pitches....

Oxygen is the third most common element in the universe. It was made millions of years after the initial Big Bang during the fusion process in millions of stars. When these stars burned out and destroyed themselves in super novas, the oxygen was released and dispersed throughout the Universe. It combined with common place gaseous hydrogen to form water. Again, there was an unimaginable amount of the stuff.

Apart from the numbers, it all seems rather simple, doesn't it? So we must also assume that apart from the water here on Earth, there is an unimaginably huge amount of water (in the form of ice) out there in the cosmos. However, there must have been, and still must be, 'Goldilocks' areas near stars where temperatures allowed it to be liquid. Any time asteroids and comets (often huge chunks of ice) are drawn into the atmosphere of a planet they heat up and the ice melts. A popular theory to explain the vast amount of liquid water on Earth attributes it to this process. You can see where I'm going now can't you. Yes, the 'waters in the firmament'.

All of a sudden the old scribes don't sound so silly, do they? Saying it's all just a coincidence, that I'm twisting reality to fit my own agenda is all very well, and of course, that is exactly what I am doing. It's called building a hypothesis. We all construct our own reality, as each one of us sees 'reality' differently.

My reality and yours are probably very similar, but they will always be just a little different in our descriptions or perspectives. To highlight this fact, I think that in *my reality,* I have stuck to my stated intention that '*I don't intend to get too involved in the details and machinations of quantum physics or theological philosophy*'. Your reality may just be a little different. If it is, I apologise, but that's just the difference in our realities....

15 GENESIS & CREATION

Looking at things from the point of view of a Genesis writing philosopher of 1400BC or thereabouts, I think it would be difficult to imagine that there was anything like life or other worlds or even the possibility of anything else in the Universe. In fact I don't suppose the concept of a 'Universe' was known about. There were just tiny lights in the sky.

Consider their dilemma. Somewhere up there, tiny lights twinkled. No matter how big a mountain you climbed, they got no closer. No matter how small the feather you held up, it always dropped to the ground when you let go, yet the tiny lights didn't fall to the ground. All the experiments you tried showed the same thing; these tiny lights were something that did not conform to the same laws of nature as everything else. Logical conclusion? They were supernatural.

Having to write up the old stories of where we came from and how the Earth was made must have been a daunting task indeed. Their view of things would be extremely limited, and very parochial. There could have been no discussion about meteorites bringing amino acids to Earth from other solar systems to 'kick start' life; no debates about how super nova's created all the elements that the Earth and its contents are made from. In fact, it must have been quite a nightmare.

There cannot be any Folk Tales that can be counted as 'race memories' such as those that probably inspired them when relating the tales of The Garden of Eden and The Original Couple. That's for the simple reason that there was no planet Earth for the folk to be on, let alone any folk to tell tales. There's no wonder that all their hypotheses are centred on Mankind and the Earth. They simply had no idea that anything else existed, so how did they manage to come up with what they did?

It was, I suppose, fairly obvious that humans had to have a supporting environment to live in, so that the planet and its biosphere must have come first. Without the detailed and fairly comprehensive knowledge about the planet and nature that is available to us today, they had to try and work out which bits came first. Oddly enough they started with the water, which they say already existed.

Holy Bible (King James Version) Genesis 1:1-8

1:1 In the beginning God created the heaven and the earth.

1:2 And the earth was without form, and void; and darkness was upon the face of the deep. And the Spirit of God moved upon the face of the waters.

1:3 And God said, Let there be light: and there was light.

1:4 And God saw the light, that it was good: and God divided the light from the darkness.

1:5 And God called the light Day, and the darkness he called Night. And the evening and the morning were the first day.

Light was described as being in existence before the creation of the Sun. Water described as existing before the creation of the Earth and what to us would be considered 'space' they seem to call 'the deep'; either that or they are referring to a large body of water not associated with Earth. There's a paradox to start with. It implies that something already existed before God began to make everything.

To people who had no knowledge of the Universe and its workings that's a very accurate statement. I wonder what they knew and just how could they know it? Guesswork? They weren't guessing though, they were making statements of fact (as far as they were concerned) It seems as though they knew quite a bit about the cosmos without even realising it, over three thousand years ago.

Next we get the famous, 'Let there be light' which some people seem to think creates light from nothing. However, consider the way suns are formed. An accumulation of rock, dust, and ice drifting through space is gathered together by gravitational attraction, then held together and added to by its own gravity which eventually becomes so strong it even attracts gases. Eventually this mass of material becomes so large and the gravitational forces so great that the material collapses in on itself and the huge pressure at the centre causes nuclear fusion to start. A pinpoint of light (as viewed from Earth) would suddenly appear in the sky without any apparent cause when the new star was born. This is a phenomenon that astronomers have witnessed for centuries, and still do today.

End of day one and still no sign of the Earth. I suppose you could argue that God made light before he made the Earth so he could see what he was doing. Maybe we should have created the 'firmament first? Why would we? From our perspective, it's just darkness, a black void. No different to the environment we are in now, except its dark and nothing to stand on. From my point of view, making the Earth first would be logical. After all, the Sun has to have something to go round, right? (*Yes, I know, Copernicus and all that, but here I'm speaking from the Bronze Age point of view!*)

Why, I wonder did the scribes do it differently? The answer of course is that they were writing down the old folk tales and legends. They had to be; otherwise their account of creation would have started with creating the Earth and building from there.

Day two brings a separation of the water 'under the firmament' (the seas) and the creation of land.

Holy Bible (King James Version) Genesis 1:6-8

1:6 And God said, Let there be a firmament in the midst of the waters, and let it divide the waters from the waters.

1:7 And God made the firmament, and divided the waters which were under the firmament from the waters which were above the firmament: and it was so.

1:8 And God called the firmament Heaven. And the evening and the morning were the second day.

There is an implication here in Genesis that the land also existed prior to God manipulating things. The dry land appears when the seas are gathered into one place. Whilst this could be just an observation that land is under the water, it doesn't do what they have set out to do, and that is to describe the actual creation of it. They make an assumption that it already existed.

Another implication appears now. If these things already existed, then we have a situation that is only describing the creation of the planet, and not of the whole of the Universe. If that is the case, then that must have happened earlier. Is verse one then, just a heading, or is it a statement that the Heavens were already made?

"In the beginning God made the Heavens and the Earth." New subject: "And the Earth was without form, and void; and darkness was upon the face of the deep." Changes things a just little bit, don't you think? It shows just how important punctuation is. It also opens up more possibilities for debate. Do we have space, with the materials for the Earth in place but not yet come together to make the planet? So the Universe is already there, the water is in it, and so is the material to build Earth.

You'll have to help me here, but is this a description by a theologian, or a description by a cosmologist? There's nothing to tell them apart. What is readily apparent though, is that either God has a different time scale to us, or the scribes were just plain wrong about the time it took.

Holy Bible (King James Version) Genesis 1:9-13

1:9 And God said, Let the waters under the heaven be gathered together unto one place, and let the dry land appear: and it was so.

1:10 And God called the dry land Earth; and the gathering together of the waters called he Seas: and God saw that it was good.

1:11 And God said, Let the earth bring forth grass, the herb yielding seed, and the fruit tree yielding fruit after his kind, whose seed is in itself, upon the earth: and it was so.

1:12 And the earth brought forth grass, and herb yielding seed after his kind, and the tree yielding fruit, whose seed was in itself, after his kind: and God saw that it was good.

1:13 And the evening and the morning were the third day.

1:14 And God said, Let there be lights in the firmament of the heaven to divide the day from the night; and let them be for signs, and for seasons, and for days, and years:

1:15 And let them be for lights in the firmament of the heaven to give light upon the earth: and it was so.

1:16 And God made two great lights; the greater light to rule the day, and the lesser light to rule the night: he made the stars also.

1:17 And God set them in the firmament of the heaven to give light upon the earth,

1:18 And to rule over the day and over the night, and to divide the light from the darkness: and God saw that it was good.

1:19 And the evening and the morning were the fourth day.

- the first day - light was created.

- the second day - the sky was created.

- the third day - dry land, seas, plants and trees were created.

- the fourth day - the Sun, Moon and stars were created.

- the fifth day - sea and creatures that fly were created.

- the sixth day – land animals and humans were created

To sum up, they got it all right apart from the fourth day. In fact if you put the statement about the fourth day second, that's a pretty accurate description of the Big Bang theory. That leaves their theory 80% in agreement with it, enough to pass a school exam. Not bad considering they managed this over three thousand years before Copernicus or Galileo started to figure it out.

The writers of Genesis refer to the sky, or space or the heavens as the 'firmament.' The word "firmament" is meant to correspond with the word 'raqia', or 'raqiya`, as used in Biblical Hebrew. About the best way to translate it is to say 'expanse'. The original Hebrew word was used to describe how, for example, a sheet of metal could be beaten to make it wider, to expand it or spread it out. A startling description when you think that cosmologists have only recently realized that the Universe is still expanding.

Many scholars in the past described the 'firmament' as a dome of some sort (the sky) that was spread out above the Earth to separate it from Heaven. We now know, of course that there is no such thing unless you consider the Earth's atmosphere to be such a thing. From here to the edge of the observable Universe is approximately 46.5 billion light years in any direction and no evidence of Heaven has yet been detected within that space. To be fair, it has to be said that there is no evidence that either the 'Dome' or Heaven does not exist within the Universe. Just not within 46.5 billion lights years of us, anyway.

Again we see that, remarkably, the old guys got it almost right. Lights in the firmament (stars) then came the local planetary system we know so well. The Universe is 13.8 billion years old and the Sun, our planet and its moon are 4.6 billion years old. The only thing we can criticize is their idea of what it was they were looking at when they gazed at the Moon or the Sun. I think we have to be somewhat lenient though; Astrophysics and the other cosmological disciplines were a little thin on the ground at the time Genesis was written. It would be another three thousand years before Galileo Galilei came up with a usable telescope in 1609 and almost three thousand four hundred years before the first exploratory space probe was launched.

Considering all they had to go on was their imagination and whatever it was that inspired them to write their masterpiece, the ancient scribes did an amazing job.

Water, water, everywhere and not a drop to drink....

Incidental to all this is the debate amongst scientists as to where all the water on Earth came from. The current theory states that after the Earth had formed, there followed millions of years during which the new planet was continually bombarded by comets and asteroids that contained water in the form of ice and which melted to form the oceans. Whilst I agree about the presence of ice, I have serious doubts about the 'bombardment'. The whole bombardment theory has come into question in cosmology circles recently.

So how did the oceans come to be formed, and where did the water come from? Isn't it self-evident? Hydrogen and Oxygen are the basic components of water. These elemental chemicals, being two of the most common, would be everywhere in the early Universe, much of it in the form of ice. Nine billion years after the Big Bang, gravity started pulling together debris from a super nova and any other items it could find, including this ice, to form the Earth. As all this stuff coalesced it began to heat up as gravity increased the pressure at the centre of the 'proto planet', so melting the ice and giving it water. After millions of years as things settled, it formed into oceans, gravity keeping it in place, and started the long haul to the situation we have today.

As our planet is near enough to the Sun to keep water (in the main) liquid, without boiling it off, we have our lovely 'blue' planet. It didn't need a tremendous bombardment of the place by comets and asteroids to bring it all here. It would have been present from the conception of the planet any way. There is no doubt that the early Earth would have been hit by asteroids, etc., as gravity would have pulled them in, but it wasn't the main source of water. That would have been present from the word 'Go'.

Archbishop Usher calculated that creation happened in 4004 BC. Others have extended his calculations and come up with a more specific time and date. 6 p.m. on Saturday 22nd of October 4004 BC. So the first Sabbath, in Christian theology, would have been Sunday the 23rd.

According to accepted modern theory, the good Archbishop's calendar seems to be just a little off by about 13 billion years or so.

I just know I'm going to get an ear bashing about this one from the Young Earth enthusiasts, but it gives us all something to talk (and write) about so it can't be a bad thing!

16 EINSTEIN & NEWTON'S THEORIES

There are certain Laws of Physics that are constant. Some of these laws are very well known. They are taught in our schools and Universities and are the staple diet of Physicists. Take for example, Einstein's Special Theory of Relativity. Don't know what I mean? Yes you do.

$E = mc^2$. E = Energy, M = Matter C = the Speed of Light in a vacuum. Simplified this law states that nothing with mass can travel faster than light.

A rather disconcerting development by that incredible piece of machinery known as the Large Hadron Collider, deep under the borders of France and Switzerland, throws Einstein's little gem into a dubious light too. Whilst examining the results of their high speed collisions of particles, the guys at CERN near Geneva have discovered that some particles called Neutrinos actually *do* travel faster than light. On September 22, 2011, they reported detection of, and I quote,

"17-GeV and 28-GeV muon neutrinos, sent 730 kilometers (454 miles) from CERN near Geneva, Switzerland to the Gran Sasso National Laboratory in Italy, traveling apparently faster than light by a factor of 2.48×10^{-5}."

Just how fast that is I hesitate to say, never mind actually calculate. But for the pedantic amongst you, here's the maths. 186,282.4 miles per second x 2.48×10^{-5} or, to put it in terms of an equation, $186,282.4 \times (2.48 \times 10^{-5})$

You work it out. I don't have a big enough calculator.

Setting aside my failure in the calculus arena, it disproves the idea that nothing with mass can travel faster than light. So can Albert go to the dunces' corner? Maybe not, for as it turned out, the guys at CERN were mistaken, but what is apparent though, is that not everything we take as fact is unshakably solid and there are always people out there challenging accepted beliefs. There is still a lot to discover, and I have a feeling that some of the revelations that are to come in the next few years are going to cause quite a commotion in academic and theological circles. Not to mention the tabloid press.

Next we have that other celebrated man of science, Sir Isaac Newton and his Third Law of Motion.

$$\sum \mathbf{F}_{a,b} = -\sum \mathbf{F}_{b,a}$$ where $F_{a,b}$ are the forces from B acting on A, and $F_{b,a}$ are the forces from A acting on B.

What do you mean; you've never heard of that one either? Yes you have. *For every action there is always an equal and opposite reaction.*

This one speaks for itself, I think. These two laws are amongst the most fundamental laws governing Physics. Isaac Newton and Albert Einstein were two of the greatest mathematicians that have ever lived. Newton's work has lasted for over three hundred years without being faulted. It is always reliable and always true, unless of course you think about the Big Bang.

We must consider that if *every* action has an *equal* and *opposite* reaction, then the creation of matter by the Big Bang (most decidedly 'an action') to form the Universe must have created anti-matter in equal quantities. So where is it? Where is the Antiverse?

Experiments, both physical and theoretical have proved that matter and anti-matter neutralise each other when they come into contact. So given that this Universe exists (has not been neutralised by anti-matter) either Newton was wrong, or we do not completely understand the basic laws of Physics that govern our Universe.

If I were a bookmaker, I wouldn't take any bets on us completely understanding the Laws of Physics. There could well be an Antiverse, somewhere (another dimension perhaps) that we cannot as yet, detect. Either way, it wrong-foots 'traditional' science and its proponents in a big way; but as with the situation existing in the field of paleoanthropology, future events and discoveries will probably sort out the confusion. I have every confidence in this.

At this point it may be worth noting that Isaac Newton's formulae are still used today, notably by NASA and other space travelers in calculating the paths satellites and interplanetary craft need to take to reach their destinations.

Not bad work for a 17th century scholar.

17 THE END OF DAYS

You have to admit that death comes to all of us eventually, but a wholesale ending of life, the Universe and time itself is something of a different animal. It's scary to say the least.

There have been many predictions of the 'End of Days'. Many of them long past and forgotten, some recently past and just a few worryingly close! Everyone from Old Mother Shipton to Isaac Newton (2034 & 2060) has had a bash at it, and as a result there are a plethora of predictions. Wikipedia for example, lists 154 examples of these predictions. My money is on Newton's 2060, extinction by Climate change.

 The Bible gives a little to go on, telling us mainly about the goings on of the anti-Christ, the Battle of Armageddon and the Archangel Michael Sounding the Trumpet to announce Judgement Day. Israfel (Hebrew: Raphael) is, according to Islamic tradition, the trumpeter who will do the job, but even so, this is the Judgement and not the end of everything earthly.

Despite what many people think, the Book of Revelations doesn't describe the end of the world. It describes the end of evil and the destruction of all things bad. It doesn't tell us how it all ends; it just presents us with a description of the events on 'Judgement Day'. There is in the Holy Qur'an though, a clue as to the end of the Earth. By now, I hope, it will come as no surprise to you, my dear reader, that we can show that it parallels science in a rather uncanny way.

Holy Qur'an Sura 70 (The Way of Ascent) Verse 8-9

70:8 On the day when the heavens shall be as molten copper
70:9 And the mountains shall be as tufts of wool

Shall we get stuck into this one? It has potential hasn't it?

What do we glean from the science publications about the end of everything? Well, our Sun, classified as a yellow dwarf star, is about half way through its life span. When all its hydrogen fuel is all used up, it will become what is known as a red giant, and will expand to such an extent that it will engulf the inner planets, including the Earth, before it collapses into a white dwarf star.

Even though its fuel will be used up, the temperature of the gaseous giant that will engulf our little home will be in excess of 1,000,000 Kelvin, maybe as much as 2,000,000 Kelvin. That's hot enough to melt anything we have here on Earth. In fact, as the Sun expands, temperatures here will rise so much that long before we are engulfed all water will boil off into space. So will our atmosphere. If you were able to view the event from the surface of the Earth, you would, as predicted in the Holy Qur'an, see the whole of the sky above your head, become one fiery molten mass as the sun started expanding.. Not long after that, the actual ground you would be standing on would start to melt. Shortly afterwards, there would be no trace of the planet that was our home for so long.

All this sounds horrific, but there's no need to worry. By the time it happens, we, as a race, will be long gone. We'll have been extinct for four billion years or so. Not even a cosmic memory.

What I have just described is not only a Qur'anic prophecy. It is what cosmologists have worked out will happen. Some 'Prophecies' are a different matter altogether, and are arrived at by many means.

Not all of them so logical as the one described above. The last doomsday event was predicted in 2012 on May 27th. One Ronald Weinland stated Jesus Christ would return on this day, with catastrophic end of time events. He also predicted that it would occur on September 29, 2011. The May 21, 2011 end times prediction made by American Christian radio host Harold Camping stated that the 'Rapture' and 'Judgment Day' would take place and that the end of the world would take place five months later on October 21, 2011. Rather embarrassingly for such a public figure, it didn't happen.

Then of course there was 21st December 2012. People connect this date to the Mayans of ancient South America who had a calendar starting sometime about the year 550BC. The calendar they used to measure the years and seasons by ended there, that is stopped on this date. However, it was not a particularly cataclysmic date, simply the end of one period, and the start of another.

The prediction given by the Mayans about what would happen at the end of this Great Cycle is described as a rebirth of this world and the beginning of an age of enlightenment. Did anyone else feel particularly enlightened?

There are also other interpretations of assorted legends, scriptures, numerological constructions and prophecies encircling this date. The Mayan calendar is still in use in Guatemala, Veracruz, Oaxaca and Chiapas, Mexico, and there are no particular fears of extinction in these places, or at least, not reported yet. Interestingly it is the time when all the planets line up in what is a fairly rare occurrence. The last one occurred on March 21, 1894 at around 23:00 GMT, when Mercury transited the Sun as seen from Venus, and Mercury and Venus both simultaneously transited the Sun as seen from Saturn.

As far as I can see, no cataclysmic world ending event took place then. The only lasting event that occurred was that Coca Cola went on sale for the first time a few days before, but even this momentous occasion had limited life threatening effects. Incidentally, as I am editing this book, today's date is the 3rd of January, 2022. No end of the World, just 'the same old same old'.

There are references to things coming to an end in the Bible, but they are not really indicative of an end to the Earth and all else.

Holy Bible (King James Version) Mathew 24:14-21

24:14 And this gospel of the kingdom shall be preached in all the world for a witness unto all nations; and then shall the end come.

24:15 When ye therefore shall see the abomination of desolation, spoken of by Daniel the prophet, stand in the holy place, (whoso readeth, let him understand:)

24:16 Then let them which be in Judaea flee into the mountains:

24:17 Let him which is on the housetop not come down to take anything out of his house: 24:18 Neither let him which is in the field return back to take his clothes.

24:19 And woe unto them that are with child, and to them that give suck in those days!

24:20 But pray ye that your flight be not in the winter, neither on the Sabbath day:

4:21 For then shall be great tribulation, such as was not since the beginning of the world to this time, no, nor ever shall be.

Even here the End is not really certain. Why would someone be advised to flee into the mountains if all was to be destroyed? It's much more likely to be advising hiding from an advancing enemy. In the continuation of this piece it says:

Holy Bible (King James Version) Mathew 24:22-27

24:22 And except those days should be shortened, there should no flesh be saved: but for the elect's sake those days shall be shortened.

24:23 Then if any man shall say unto you, Lo, here is Christ, or there; believe it not.

24:24 For there shall arise false Christs, and false prophets, and shall shew great signs and wonders; insomuch that, if it were possible, they shall deceive the very elect.

24:25 Behold, I have told you before.

24:26 Wherefore if they shall say unto you, Behold, he is in the desert; go not forth: behold, he is in the secret chambers; believe it not.

24:27 For as the lightning cometh out of the east, and shineth even unto the west; so shall also the coming of the Son of man be.

These are the same signs of the Day of Judgement as repeated in The Book of Revelations. A more hopeful (?) passage comes next.

Holy Bible (King James Version) Mathew 24:28-31

24:28 For whosoever the carcase is, there will the eagles be gathered together.

24:29 Immediately after the tribulation of those days shall the sun be darkened, and the moon shall not give her light, and the stars shall fall from heaven, and the powers of the heavens shall be shaken:

24:30 And then shall appear the sign of the Son of man in heaven: and then shall all the tribes of the earth mourn, and they shall see the Son of man coming in the clouds of heaven with power and great glory.

24:31 And he shall send his angels with a great sound of a trumpet, and they shall gather together his elect from the four winds, from one end of heaven to the other.

So Michael or Azrael will be sounding the trumpet, and the stars shall fall from the heaven, and the Sun and Moon cease to shine. This is the Second Coming, the arrival of the Messiah preceding the Day of Judgement. Lots of detail, but there is something conspicuous by its absence, a date. Not that the Bible doesn't recognise the passing of the Earth. Up next is the clue.

Holy Bible (King James Version) Mathew 24:32-36

24:32 Now learn a parable of the fig tree; When his branch is yet tender, and putteth forth leaves, ye know that summer is nigh:

24:33 So likewise ye, when ye shall see all these things, know that it is near, even at the doors.

24:34 Verily I say unto you, This generation shall not pass, till all these things be fulfilled.

24:35 Heaven and earth shall pass away, but my words shall not pass away.

24:36 But of that day and hour knoweth no man, no, not the angels of heaven, but my Father only.

According to this passage we will not be told when it will happen. Sorry boys and girls, it's a Divine secret. The problem is that two verses earlier we are told that the generation alive at the time would still be there when these things happened.

This is why all the pundits looking back on events (hindsight is always 20-20) say it refers to the Roman sacking of Jerusalem and the destruction of the Jewish state as a whole, not the end of the world.

Thinking about this passage, I can't help wondering if Judgement Day has been and gone. After all, these prophecies were told to and pertained to, the Jews of two thousand years ago. It strikes me that their Judges were the Romans and that the end of their time came about. It wasn't until 1948 that they regained any sort of control over the same lands, and even now their hold on things is tenuous. Maybe as God said in Genesis:

Holy Bible (King James Version) Genesis 6:3

6:3 And the LORD said, My spirit shall not always strive with man, for that he also is flesh: yet his days shall be an hundred and twenty years.

This is a rather interesting statement. Despite several individuals claiming to have done so, no one has actually been proven to live past this age, which makes me wonder about the Biblical claims that many individuals lived to be several hundred years of age. It is all very well to make the claim, but actual experience dictates otherwise.

Has God actually given up on us? Has His spirit finished 'striving' with man? Have we been abandoned to our fate, whatever it may be? It rather looks as though we're on our own.

"Goodnight, goodbye and may your God go with you."

A VERY INCOMPLETE GLOSSARY OF TERMS & EXPRESSIONS

1.Acid Rain Caused by emissions of carbon dioxide, sulphur dioxide and nitrogen oxides which react with the water molecules in the atmosphere to produce acids that fall as rain.

2.Anthropology Study of humanity.

3.Archaeologist Student of human history from the development of the first stone tools

4.Atheist Person who doesn't believe in a God.

5.Agadir Provincial port town of Agadir province in southwest Morocco.

6.Aggadah Traditions providing the authoritative interpretation of the Jewish Written Law. In this context, the widely held view in Rabbinic literature is that the aggadah is in fact a medium for the transmission of fundamental teachings.

7.Aqaba: Gulf of Eastern branch of northern Red Sea.

8.Babylon Akkadian city-state (founded in 1867 BC) of ancient Mesopotamia, (Iraq), about 85 kilometres (55 mi) south of Baghdad.

9.Baculum Bone that stiffens mammalian penis.

10.Big Bang Current theory as to the origin of the Universe and everything in it. Nobel prize winner, Georges Lemaître (17 Jul 1894 - 20 Jun 1966) a Belgian priest, first proposed what would become the Big Bang theory. In 1927, he published his article *"A Homogeneous Universe of Constant Mass and Increasing Radius accounting for the Radial Velocity of Extra Galactic Nebulae."* It does not explain any state of existence prior to it.

11.Blue Planet   Euphemism for Planet Earth, as it is predominantly blue when viewed from Space.

12.Brass Monkeys   English colloquial vulgarity.   *'Cold enough to freeze the balls off a brass monkey'.*   Implies very cold weather.

13.Bronze Age   Period of time Homo s.sapien used copper and bronze tools before developing the ability to smelt iron ore.   This term has cannot be applied in Africa outside the Nile Valley, as most of Africa proceeded straight from 'Stone Age' to 'Iron Age'.

14.Charles Darwin   (12 Feb 1809-19 Apr 1882) Naturalist and Geologist.   Originator of the Theory of Evolution by Natural Selection.

15.Chromosome   an organized structure of DNA and protein found in cells. It is a single piece of coiled DNA containing many genes.

15a. DNA Deoxyribonucleic acid. Commonly referred to as 'the building blocks of life'.

16.Cool Dude Person who is unfazed by events.

17.Dinosaurs Extinct diverse group of animals of the clade and superorder Dinosauria. They appeared in the Triassic period at least 230 million years ago and were the dominant terrestrial reptilians for 135 million years.

18.Dogma Beliefs that are accepted without reason or evidence.

19.Ecosystem Natural self-sustaining environment that supports life.

20.Einstein: Albert (14 March 1879 – 18 April 1955) German-Jewish theoretical physicist. Developed the theory of general relativity, effecting a revolution in physics. Regarded as the father of modern physics and one of the most prolific intellects in human history. Received the 1921 Nobel Prize in Physics, especially for his discovery of the law of the photoelectric effect. The latter was pivotal in establishing quantum theory within physics. Developed his Special Theory of Relativity. Applied the general theory of relativity to model the structure of the universe as a whole. Einstein published more than 300 scientific papers along with over 150 non-scientific works. His great intelligence and originality have made the word "Einstein" synonymous with genius.

21.Fossil Remains of dead plants and animals, such as the bones and teeth of vertebrates, mineralized after spending extensive periods of time buried in the ground.

22.Gender Sexual attributes of a creature, i.e. male or female.

23.Gene Name given to certain sections of DNA.

24.Genus A low-level taxonomic rank used in the biological classification of living and fossil organisms..

25.God a.k.a. Elohim, Yahweh, Allah. Deity of Abrahamic religions.

26.Goldilocks (zone or period) place or time that was or is warm enough to allow water to be liquid, and support life.

27.Great Unknown Euphemism for outer space.

28.Hadith Traditions providing the authoritative interpretation of Islamic Law.

29.Henry Ford (Jul 30, 1863-Apr 7, 1947) Inventor of the <u>moving</u> assembly line, and major motor car manufacturer.

30.Holocene Period of time which began at the end of the Pleistocene (around 12,000 to 14000 years ago) and continues to the present.

31.Holy Bible Holy scripture of Christian religions.

32.Holy Land Palestine and Jordan. Lands frequented by Biblical characters.

33.Holy Qur'an (Koran) Holy scripture of Islamic religion.

34.Holy Trinity Christian concept of the attributes of God

(Father, Son and Holy Spirit).

35.Hominin a.k.a Hominid. Member of the genus Homo.

36.Homo 'Man'. The binominal name *Homo s.sapien* is due to Carl Linnaeus 23 May 1707 – 10 January 1778), Homo as a genus of the order Primates is first recorded 1797.

37.Horn of Africa term used to describe the Somalia Peninsular. Denotes region containing the countries of Eritrea, Djibouti, Ethiopia and Somalia.

38.Hybrid Combination of two different species, e.g. Liger, cross between a lion and a tiger.

39.Iron Age Period of time Homo s.sapien used iron, as opposed to steel tools. Earliest examples in Africa 1200BC. Ended about 300AD.

40.Ka'ba Cuboid building in the centre of the Great Mosque in Mecca, Saudi Arabia. Built by Abraham and the most sacred site of Islam.

41.Kelvin primary unit of temperature measurement in the physical sciences, but is often used in conjunction with the degree Celsius, which has the same magnitude. Absolute zero at 0 K is –273.15 °C (–459.67 °F).

42.King James Version EarlyTtanslation into English of the Holy Bible using Hebrew and Aramaic sources.

43.Knuckle Dragger English slang to denote a person who is ape like, mentally slow. Refers to ape's ability to walk on all fours, using its hands as front feet.

44.KT Event (Cretaceous-Tertiary Mass Extinction event) happened 65 million years ago: 6 mile wide (10km) asteroid collided with Earth, killing over 70% of life, including the dinosaurs.

45.Kurd Individual of the Kurdish people. Kurdistan includes adjacent parts of Iran, Iraq, Syria, and Turkey.

46.L'Ayoun Capital city of Western Sahara, effectively a province of Morocco.

47.Layman Amateur, unqualified practitioner not trained or qualified in a particular discipline. Notably in religious context.

48.Mesopotamia Ancient name meaning 'the Land Between the Rivers'. (Tigris and Euphrates). Partly in today's Iraq and partly in Syria.

49.Middle Ages General term used to describe period of time between 5th and 15th centuries.

50.Millennia (plural) period of one thousand years; Millennium singular.

51.Newton: Sir Isaac (25 December 1642 – 20 March 1727) President of Royal Society, built the first practical reflecting telescope, wrote Principia Mathematica, described universal gravitation and the three laws of motion. Described the makeup of light, and is generally thought to be one of the greatest scientists and mathematicians who ever lived. His other achievements are too great and numerous to list here. In Newton's eyes, worshipping Christ as God was idolatry, to him the fundamental sin.

52.Pagan Person who worships natural phenomena, or 'Mother Earth'.

53.Palaeoanthropology The study of ancient human life.

54.Palaeontology The study of prehistoric life. It includes the study of fossils to determine organisms' evolution and interactions with each other and their environments.

55.Phylum General grouping of organisms based on general specialization of body plan, as well as developmental or internal organizations.

56.Primate Mammal of the order Primates. Includes monkeys, gorillas chimpanzees, orang-utans and humans.

57.Q.E.D Abbreviated form of 'quod erat demonstrandum', which translates as 'which was to be demonstrated' and used to indicate the completion of the proof

58.Raging Planet American documentary television series that focuses on natural disasters such as hurricanes, tsunamis and earthquakes.

59.Ras Mohammed Headland at the junction of the Red Sea Gulf of Suez and Gulf of Aqaba.

60.Russian Roulette The ultimate game of chance in which the players place a single bullet in a revolver, spin the cylinder, then take turns in holding the muzzle against their head and pulling the trigger.

61.Russian Steppes Savannah in central Russia.

62.Saharan Pump Theory Following wet periods when the Sahara is lush and green, many animals inhabit the area. Later when it reverts to desert conditions (usually as a result of the retreat of the West African Monsoon southwards) Flora and fauna previously widespread retreat northwards to the Atlas Mountains or southwards into West Africa, or eastwards into the Nile Valley and thence either south-east to the Ethiopian Highlands and Kenya or north-east across the Sinai into Asia.

63.Savannah Extensive grasslands with sparse tree cover.

64.Sexual Dimorphism Differences between males and females of the same species e.g. size, colouring.

65.Singularity a situation where matter is forced to be compressed to an (infinitely?) small point. Please refer to Penrose–Hawkins definition. Too difficult for me!

66.Sixpence (colloquial: Tanner) Nickel-silver coin worth one fortieth of a pound (Stirling) from 1551 until 1971.

67.Smithsonian Institution. 19 museums, a Zoo and research centres in Washington DC, USA. World's largest museum organisation.

68.Soviet Union U.S.S.R Communist Russian empire. World's largest state from 1922-1991

69.Space Age Started with Russian satellite 'Sputnik One' Oct. 4 1957. Still in progress!

70.Spud English slang word for potato.

71.Sumer Group of City States in northern Mesopotamia. Citizens known as 'Sumerians'.

72.Steam Age Period of time Homo s.sapien used (predominantly) steam powered machinery. Started 1698 with Thomas Savery's water pump. Generally considered to have ended in the 1960's with demise of steam powered locomotives.

73.Stone Age Period of time Homo species used stone tools before developing metallurgy skills. First stone tools appear in fossil records about 2.9 million years ago, and the first metal tools appeared about 5-6,000 years BC

74.Suez: Gulf of Western branch of northern Red Sea

75.Theologian Religious scholar.

76.Universe The Cosmos. The space containing the Earth and everything else. The sum total of all matter that exists.

77.Vitruvian Man The correlations of ideal human proportions with geometry, described by the ancient Roman architect Vitruvius in Book III of his treatise 'De Architectura'. Vitruvius described the human figure as being the principal source of proportion among the Classical orders of architecture.

78.Zohar   Foundational work in the literature of Jewish mystical thought known as Kabbalah.

ABOUT THE AUTHOR

Peter Leadley was born in Yorkshire, England, in 1950.

For his first ten years he lived with his grandparents; his grandmother being the daughter of an Anglican 'high church' vicar. His grandmother gave him a good start in his quest for knowledge of the truth about God and religion.

At the age of 42 he embraced Islam and studied the principals that guide Muslims.

In 1994 he spent six months as a volunteer truck driver for Convoy of Mercy, a logistics supply NGO in the Bosnian war zone, being the 'Tail End Charlie' and truck boss of the convoy that broke the Siege of Sarajevo in April of that year.

Since 2001 he has lived in the Netherlands, during which time he visited many of the places mentioned in this book. His Dutch friends consider him to be an archetypal Englishman.

He retired at 60 years of age and began to research and write Adam & Eve & the Big Bang.

He has been married five times, has four children, six grandchildren and two great grandchildren.